AWESOME ATHLETIC PERFORMANCE

ACHIEVING PEAK PERFORMANCE WITH HYPNOSIS AND NLP

LAURA KING

1375 N. Killian Drive
Lake Park, FL 33403
877.482.7352
www.summitpress.net

To buy books in quantity for
corporate use or incentives,
call (877) 482-7352 or email
laurakinginfo@gmail.com

Credits:
Layout: Jonathan Gullery / RJ Communications

ISBN: 978-0-9826613-7-6   Paperback
ISBN: 978-0-9826613-9-0   mobi
ISBN: 978-0-9826613-8-3   eBook

Printed in the United States of America

First printing, 2014

AWESOME
ATHLETIC
PERFORMANCE

This book belongs
To : The

Russell
Family

CONTENTS

INTRODUCTION

HELLO, my name is Laura King. I am a Certified Hypnotist, a Certified Sports Hypnotist and the founder of Summit Performance Center in Wellington, Florida. I also have my Master's Practitioner Certification in Neuro-Linguistic Psychology. When I began studying hypnosis over 30 years ago, I had no idea that my passion for helping people and my love of sports would one day come together. I'm proud to say I now offer a comprehensive self-hypnosis program designed to help athletes of all levels reach their goals.

Hypnosis is a proven, time-tested way to help you achieve all of your goals. Millions of people have benefited from its power to help them make positive changes in their lives, including notables such as: Tiger Woods, Albert Einstein, Jacqueline Kennedy-Onassis, Henry Ford, Muhammed Ali, Kevin Costner, and Wolfgang Amadeus Mozart.

Hypnosis can help you transform bad habits such as smoking, eating unhealthy foods, or biting your fingernails, into good ones like saying thank you, exercising, taking better care of yourself, and being more aware of what you need to do for yourself. It can help you turn your negative or sad feelings into positive, happy ones. It can help you effortlessly focus on almost anything in your life that you would like to change, while leaving you unburdened by analytical or pessimistic thoughts.

And of course, it can help you improve your athletic performance, from the inside out. A professional coach, trainer or pro can help

you improve your skills and techniques by guiding you through physical rehearsal, and hypnosis can improve your confidence and focus
by guiding you through mental rehearsal. Hypnosis will help you
get more out of your chosen sport by helping you easily recall any
acquired skills, easily get rid of your past fears, sharpen your concentration, and believe in yourself so that you can achieve peak performance.
You can eliminate any mental or subconscious barriers and maximize
your potential.

You'll find that hypnosis does more than help you have a better
golf swing, better time in that pesky swim leg of the triathlon, or a
more accurate pitch or serve. It helps you understand yourself better.
In fact, it helps you become your real self. When you start to relax,
the things you do to prevent you from being your real self go away
and what's left is your real self. The chatter stops. You become more
comfortable in your own skin and with your abilities. You become
more comfortable with your *self*.

Because what's inside you and what's outside of you are equally
important to achieving optimal performance, if you currently take
lessons from a pro, don't stop. Neither this book nor The 6 Keys to
Awesome Athletic Performance series is a replacement for your pro's
technical know-how. Instead, it's complementary—it helps you apply
your coach's tips much more quickly, thoroughly, and confidently. It
allows the brain to actually do what it is being taught, effortlessly.

My guess is that if you're reading this book you're a person who
wants life to be full of peak experiences, and especially peak athletic
performance. This book, with or without the CDs, will start you (or
further your progress) on a journey to the place inside your mind that
can create any experience—any future—you desire, one thought at a
time.

I organized this book the same way I organize my seminars: by first
explaining the tools I use—Hypnosis; Neuro-Linguistic Programming

(NLP); The Laws of the Universe and The Natural Laws of the Mind—and then by showing you how to combine them to produce peak athletic performance, no matter what your current level is. I've included real-life stories to illustrate how hypnosis and self-hypnosis have helped my clients achieve higher levels of performance than they previously thought were possible (and that thought process was usually a big part of the problem, but we'll get into that later).

The 6 Keys to Awesome Athletic Performance program is a series that allows every type of athlete and every level of athlete to experience the benefits of hypnosis in the privacy and comfort of their homes. The underlying principle behind the series is that the more relaxed and confident you are as a player or runner or swimmer, the more you enjoy what you're doing. And the more you enjoy yourself, the more successful you will be. Each of the keys I discuss in this book is based on one of the CDs in The 6 Keys to Awesome Athletic Performance program and targets a critical area of your subconscious mind to create quick, easy, effortless, positive change. You will learn how to hypnotize yourself to achieve the same results you'd achieve if you were listening to the CDs or if I were sitting across from you.

The subconscious mind is most receptive to positive messages when in a state of deep, comfortable relaxation. In this state you can take your performance to the next level by making yourself confident, fearless, and focused, by making suggestions to your subconscious. In your first self-hypnosis session, *Calm, Cool, & Collected*, you'll learn breathing techniques that cultivate deep physical and mental relaxation. Muscle tension is replaced by peace and harmony, producing smooth, effortless, and relaxed body movements for a more pleasurable playing experience.

Positive Self-Talk will help you conquer your enemy within. We're all our own worst enemies, as we are capable of creating and/or perpetuating a lifetime of negativity all by ourselves, beginning with that gray stuff between our ears. Replacing your negative inner monologue with empowering, confident, uplifting language is a crucial step in the retraining of your brain.

The third self-hypnosis session in the series puts you on the path to success by helping you improve your powers of concentration. Your ability to concentrate is bolstered by exercises that help you increase your self-awareness and self-discipline. *Gaining Concentration* gives you the ability to compete despite the presence of potential distractions around you or in your mind.

There are very few athletes in any sport who have never experienced some form of performance anxiety. These fears are often amplified when there is any kind of audience and all eyes (or even some of the eyes) are on you. And you probably already have enough anxiety from your own thoughts about your performance and its outcome. *Release of Performance Anxiety*, the fourth session in The 6 Keys to Awesome Athletic Performance series, uses mental imagery to help you replace feelings of anxiety with feelings of being a winner. When you release performance anxiety you're able to gain satisfaction from effortlessly reproducing the swing, form, kick, serve, or whatever else you've rehearsed in your mind. Though you cannot control the outcome, you *can* control your mental rehearsal.

You can also shift your mental state from terrified to intrepid, and the fifth CD, *Mastering Fear*, demonstrates how you can control what's going on in your head and make it work for you rather than against you.

The final self-hypnosis session is called *Achieving Peak Performance* and is based on two key concepts. First, visualization is essential to success. All great athletes rehearse their performances in their minds to create the results they desire. Through the repetition of hypnotic suggestion, you can communicate with your subconscious mind and program yourself for success. Second, peak performance is achieved only after you are able to build confidence, poise, and self-image.

The most important concept I wish for you to understand is that the reason for the success of my clients isn't me—it's them. Hypnosis is something you allow to happen; you technically do it to yourself. All hypnosis is really self-hypnosis. You have within you—right now—the power to change almost anything you want about your thoughts and behavior.

How to Use This Book

Part I gives you an overview of hypnosis, NLP, The Laws of the Universe and The Natural Laws of the Mind—the tools I use to produce *Awesome Athletic Performance*. They're at the core of the effectiveness of what I do with my clients. My intention isn't to provide a thorough explanation of the history of the principles I base my practice on. If that's something you desire, any bookstore, and of course the Internet, will have oodles of books on them. My purpose is to briefly explain them and why they work so well.

Part II explains the *6 Keys* in detail, including many examples from my own experience and from my clients' experiences. I'm sure you'll find yourself somewhere in the stories, as I have yet to see a new problem or mistake.

Part III provides a step-by-step process for setting and achieving your goals using self-hypnosis. At the end of Part III, you will have a customized plan, including a timeline, action steps, and affirmations, that will guide you to achieving the outcomes you desire.

Enjoy your journey, and remember that awesome athletic perfor-mance is just a thought away.

Laura King
Palm Beach Gardens, Florida
December 2013

PART 1
THE TOOLS FOR CHANGING YOUR BEHAVIOR

CHAPTER 1

WHAT IS HYPNOSIS, AND WHY DO YOU NEED IT?

HYPNOSIS has a fascinating history and evokes varying images and feelings. Some people imagine a man in a theater making people quack like ducks, some think a hypnotist can make them reveal all their secrets, and some think it's all a bunch of malarkey.

The truth is hypnosis can help you understand who you are now, and help you discover who you want to become. Best of all, once you discover who you want to be, it can help you become that person. It can help you change your bad habits into good ones and transform your negative feelings into positive ones, and it can produce these changes effortlessly. And it can help you become a person who knows how to instantly access their inner tools to create peak athletic performance.

One common misconception about hypnosis centers on your degree of awareness during a session. When hypnosis is used for therapeutic purposes, as opposed to a stage show, you're aware and in control the entire time. If you're seeking hypnosis as a way to improve your life, your hypnotist has no magical power and cannot control you or make you do things you don't want to do. Hypnosis is a completely voluntary act wherein you always remain conscious; you're always aware and able to hear, to talk, and to make decisions.

Hypnosis is a collaboration; it's a partnership. You decide what you want to work on, you make a choice to use hypnosis and maintain a positive attitude about it (more on that later), and your hypnotherapist (or your self-hypnosis CDs) guides you to what you want. Both an expert hypnotherapist and a receptive individual are necessary in order for the process to be successful.

How do I know I can be hypnotized?

The vast majority of people of normal intelligence can be hypnotized and you can only be hypnotized if you want to be and you willingly follow the hypnotist's instructions. There are definitely people who are more or less hypnotizable than others, and also more or less willing than others. But most people fall somewhere in the middle once they understand what it's about and realize that it's safe and it's going to help them. They comfortably go into a state of relaxation and hypnosis and are receptive to the suggestions of the hypnotist.

Again, think of your hypnotist as a collaborator. If you choose to follow your hypnotist's instructions, you'll be guided into a wonderful, relaxed state of focus and awareness. And afterwards, you'll remember everything that happened. All hypnosis is self-hypnosis, and all hypnosis is just complete relaxation. But you must decide you are receptive to using hypnosis, and you must choose a hypnotist who is well trained and ethical as your collaborator. You must have complete trust that your hypnotist is invested in you and your goals.

Do you wave a pocket watch and say things like, "You are getting sleeeepy?"

Actually, many hypnotherapists use the pocket watch, but I

choose to use my voice as my only tool. The sound of my voice has always worked flawlessly for me in getting my clients into a state of hypnosis. I'll describe my induction technique more in a bit.

How do I know I've been hypnotized?

At the time, you probably won't think you were hypnotized at all. Most people realize that they were indeed hypnotized after they've noticed how relaxed they are and after they've seen the desired change(s) in their behavior and performance. If you're using the CDs, after you've heard my voice several times, eventually just the sound of it will hypnotize you. If you were in my office, I'd know that you were hypnotized because you would give me three signs: 1) your eyelids would flutter (REM); 2) your breath would slow; and 3) the whites of your eyes would get red or pink. To validate that I was correct, I'd ask you to clasp your hands tightly together. Then I'd tell you that you wouldn't be able to separate them because they'd been glued together, and that the harder you'd try to separate them, the more bonded they'd become. Finally, I'd ask you to try to separate them, and you wouldn't be able to. Alternatively, I'd ask you to close your eyes, and then I'd tell you that your eyelids were so heavy that you wouldn't be able to open them. The harder you'd try, the heavier they'd get, I'd tell you. When I'd ask you to try to open them, you wouldn't be able to.

What will I feel like when I'm being hypnotized?

I can't say for sure, because we're all different and respond to stimulus in our own unique ways. Some people tell me they don't feel any different. Others tell me that they feel very relaxed and heavy, like a lead weight. And then there are the lucky ones who feel like they are floating on a cloud and they feel better than ever before.

How is hypnosis different than meditation?

The goal of hypnosis is to change behavior through direct suggestion. It's the reprogramming of the brain. Though there are myriad different types of meditation, their goal is the quieting of the mind, the concentration on a specific state (e.g., compassion, forgiveness, love, death), or the relaxation of the entire being. Though a change in your mental or even physical state is involved, the goal of meditation, per se, is not to alter your behavior.

How is hypnosis different than therapy?

Assuming there's no hypnosis involved, therapy appeals only to the conscious mind. It enlists the help of the intellect to solve problems and relieve stress. When you appeal to the conscious mind you can undoubtedly gain a lot of knowledge. But the more reasoning and intellectualizing you engage in, the greater the tendency to rationalize, to develop alibis, and to prevent the subconscious from changing your behavior, including your athletic performance.

What if I get stuck during hypnosis and can't get out?

You can never get stuck in hypnosis because you have the power to emerge yourself at any time. All you have to do is tell yourself that you are emerging. Remember, all hypnosis is really just self-hypnosis. You're always in charge.

Why do I need hypnosis?

When you're in a hypnotic state you can easily make positive changes because your subconscious mind is more open to suggestions for change. To understand how and why that's so, it's important to understand some things about how your mind works.

But first, a few tidbits about the history of hypnosis . . .

- Hypnosis is older than recorded history. Thousands of years ago, primitive people in Africa and Australia used chanting, drums, and the fixation of their eyes to achieve the state we now know as hypnosis. They were able to effortlessly perform amazing physical feats and easily endure situations that would ordinarily cause excruciating physical pain.

- For 200 years, scientists, physicians, surgeons, theorists, and researchers have been using and studying what we now call hypnosis.

- What we now call hypnosis originated with an 18th century Australian healer named Franz Anton Mesmer (1734-1815), who believed the magnetic pull of the heavenly bodies influences the human body. His thesis at Vienna University, where he studied theology and medicine, was entitled, "The Influence of the Planets on the Human Body." Mesmer's theory was called animal magnetism, and later, mesmerism, and his methods were theatrical and profoundly uncon-ventional. For example, the venue for his treatments was a darkened hall where the patient was virtually submerged in an oak tub filled with water, and objects such as broken glass, iron filings, and empty bottles were placed in the tub. The tub's cover was pierced with iron rods, which the patient would wave over the diseased parts of the body.

- Though Mesmer produced astounding results and healed many people without medicine or surgery, mesmerism was widely criticized. He was soon associated with the occult and accused of flagrant charlatanism, as his experiments blended astrology and metaphysics in a way that was not appreci-ated at the time. He didn't get the approval of the scientific community, but his efforts were not for naught. None other than Benjamin Franklin, the American Ambassador in France at the time, was on the committee that investigated him, and Franklin thought Mesmer's claims and abilities were worthy of further consideration.

- In the early 1800s, several pioneering Frenchmen continued investigating and experimenting with mesmerism. Eventually, in 1843, it was a well-respected English surgeon named James Braid (1795-1860) who used the term "hypnotism" and differentiated it from mesmerism. Braid believed there was nothing paranormal about hypnosis, and he demonstrated that it's a state that can easily be induced by fixing the patient's eyes on a single object.

- Hypnosis was successfully used as anesthesia for thousands of operations before chloroform and ether were discovered and later (and very slowly) accepted for use during surgery.

- Hypnosis was widely used by physicians and psychologists during World War I and World War II to treat battle fatigue and mental disorders resulting from war.

- Hypnosis is now frequently used in medicine and dentistry to prepare clients for procedures they are anxious or fearful about, and also to decrease nausea and pain and decrease the need for pain medication. It is also used for psychiatric/ psychological disorders, to alleviate the suffering from incest, rape and physical abuse, and to treat high blood pressure, sleep disorders and sexual dysfunction. Even allergies and asthma can be treated with hypnosis.

- Hypnosis not only helps people lose significant weight, it helps them keep it off.

- Actors Bruce Willis and James Earl Jones both used hypnosis to successfully treat their debilitating stuttering.

- As I'm sure you've heard, smoking cessation is possible with hypnosis. You may recall Ellen DeGeneres stopped smoking by using hypnosis and had her hypnotist on her show for a demonstration. Hypnosis (both on a group level and individual) has been shown to be more effective than drug interventions for smoking cessation and three times as effective as the nicotine patch and 15 times as effective as willpower.

- Hypnosis is used by people from all walks of life and of all ages (even children, with the approval and supervision of their parents) who are interested in improving their performance at work, in school, on the tennis court, on the golf course, or even at cheerleading. I'm sure you've also heard that many professional athletes use hypnosis to improve their performance and their ability to stay in the zone. Tiger Woods, Andre Agassi, Hall of Famer Rod Carew, and basketball coach Phil Jackson have all benefitted from the use of hypnosis. If you want to improve your performance at anything, hypnosis is a great tool.

MODERN HYPNOSIS

The most influential figure in modern medical hypnosis is thought to be Dr. Milton H. Erickson (1901-1980), the founding president of the American Society of Clinical Hypnosis, who had degrees in both medicine and psychology. Erickson used myriad verbal strategies and guided imageries to help his patients access their inner abilities to heal themselves and optimize their performance in many areas of their lives. One of the most profound of Erickson's contributions was that the subconscious could be indirectly accessed to promote healing. In other words, when he was hypnotizing his patients, he didn't tell them what they were feeling (e.g., you are getting sleepy). Instead, he suggested to them that they might consider feeling a certain way (e.g. "perhaps you might notice that you are feeling sleepy"). Erickson was able to put someone into a deep trance in a short period of time without mentioning the word "hypnosis" at all.

This might not seem to be a big difference, but it is; it puts the patients in a position of personal control and freedom. They can choose whether to, for instance, get sleepy. When we feel a sense of control, relaxing and accessing the subconscious is easier and more likely to occur.

Erickson also pioneered the use of verbal strategies that are very closely related to Neuro-Linguistic Programming (NLP). He realized that the way the mind processes certain words, combinations of words, words with multiple meanings, and even pauses and longer silences, profoundly affects what the mind thinks and what the body does. This will become clear in the next chapter, but for now, understand that Erickson demonstrated that language is a profoundly persuasive tool. It can engender positive change/negative change, it can increase/decrease performance, it can increase/decrease physical and mental pain, and it can even help an individual consciously control bodily functions that are not usually under our control (e.g., heart rate).

Erickson was at the forefront of clinical study and research demonstrating that the subconscious can be responsible for many of our psychological problems and much of our dysfunctional behavior. He amassed a group of zealous followers dedicated to furthering his work, and when he passed away in 1980, those followers started schools of applied psychology based on his work.

Since then, there has been a veritable explosion in hypnosis programs and centers for hypnosis as research study after study has demonstrated just how effective it is in altering the human experience and the mind/body connection.

As we'll see in the next chapter, Neuro-Linguistic Programming (NLP) is one of the schools of applied psychology influenced by the Ericksonian model of hypnosis and hypnotherapy. Once you hear about how simple and logical it is, you'll understand why I use it to structure my hypnosis sessions.

Giving Credit to Dave Elman

At the beginning of this section, I stated that Erickson is *thought* to be the most influential figure in modern medical hypnosis. That's because there's another figure who, in my opinion, is just as influential, yet rarely gets the credit he deserves. His name was Dave Elman (1900-1967), and he wasn't a physician or psychologist. In fact, he had no medical training whatsoever; he was a Vaudevillian who later became a musician and radio producer. He was also a self-taught expert in hypnosis who began sharing his expertise—primarily with physicians, surgeons, and psychiatrists—in the late 1940s and became famous for his rapid induction technique. Some say that Milton Erickson learned much of what he later would be known for from Dave Elman.

Giving Credit to Dorothy Gates

Dorothy Gates, Ph.D. was a pioneer in the world of hypnosis. In addition to developing her own company, called Spectra Dynamics, she was an internationally recognized lecturer in the field of self-hypnosis. Dr. Gates also founded the Sunnyside Foundation, a non-profit organization providing research and scholarship in the development of inner resources.

Dorothy has been my guardian angel for most of my life. Most of what I know I learned from her, and the reason I feel so compelled to help others is because she helped me so much, so many times. Thanks to her teachings and guidance, I am who I am today. My only hope for this lifetime is that I have a fraction of the impact on others that Dorothy had on me.

THE BRAIN AND THE MIND:
WHERE THE ACTION IS

The brain and the mind have different jobs. In order to understand how hypnosis works, you need to understand what's occurring inside your head as you use self-hypnosis in the process of healing your body and achieving your desired state of wellness.

The Brain

The brain is a physical, tangible thing. It's about three pounds, it has about 86 billion neurons and it's spongy. You know where it is and roughly what it looks like. It has properties that dictate how it functions, and we know what those properties are. One of them—the one that is most important for hypnosis—is the brainwave.

The level that your brain is operating at dictates how you feel, how you behave and how you perform. The hypnotic state is attained by taking your brain from Beta, which it's probably in right now, to the Alpha state to relax and enter your subconscious mind and alter your behavior, and then even to the Theta state, where you are so highly suggestible that even deeper programming can occur, in addition to changes in memory and physical perception. Here's a brief summary of the brainwaves and what occurs at each of the four states of consciousness that are important to a discussion about hypnosis.

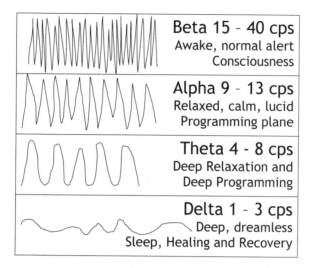

Beta

- The center for logic, analyzing and reasoning.
- In Beta, you are awake, normal, and alert. This state of consciousness is characterized by sense-experiences: sight, sound, smell, taste and touch.
- When measuring this state of consciousness on an EEG (electroencephalogram) or other biofeedback machine, we find that it registers at 15-40 cycles per second. That's fast.
- At its maximum capacity, Beta comprises only 12% of your total being. Relying on Beta is like relaying on a moped to pull a tank.
- The high level of brain activity in Beta significantly affects brain's ability to: store information (memory), access creativity, focus and concentrate on the workings of the physical body.
- You spend about 90% of the day with your brain in Beta, but when you get stuck there, tension and negative thinking usually result. The more stressed you feel, the faster your

brain will go, and the less likely you are to achieve Alpha, which is where you'd rather be. You'll see glimpses of where you can go and what you can do, but they'll be fleeting.

Alpha

- Alpha is the strongest, most prominent brain rhythm.
- Alpha is the optimal state for your brain when you need to be focused and sharp.
- When measuring this state of consciousness on a biofeedback machine, we find that its frequency registers at a 9-15 cycles per second.
- The brain's biochemistry is completely balanced in Alpha and the brain functions at optimal level.
- Decision-making is at its peak in Alpha.
- This level is necessary in order to achieve behavior modification. In Alpha, you are relaxed, calm and lucid. This is the programming plane, where you can add new programs and delete old ones. You can also control your dreams while here.
- Alpha is where you are during the first 30 minutes when you're falling asleep, but you're not quite asleep.

Theta

- Theta is where you are after the first 30 minutes when you're falling asleep, but before the point when you're sleeping deeply.
- Active dreaming takes place in Theta.
- Theta is the level achieved when you're being hypnotized by someone else, such as during hypnotherapy or stage hypnosis. It's very difficult to reach Theta through

self-hypnosis. This is where you can create hallucinations, amnesia, physical perception changes and deep programming.

- Theta is characterized by deep relaxation and clear mental imagery. This is where you aim to go when you meditate. You can experience painless surgery, dentistry and childbirth in Theta.
- Brainwave frequency is measured at 5-9 cycles per second. That's pretty slow.
- In Theta, tasks are so automatic that you aren't consciously aware of what you are doing, such as when you drive home and have no recollection of the actual drive.

Delta

- Delta is characterized by deep, dreamless sleep. The body is completely at rest.
- This is where healing and recovery take place.
- The brain operates at 1-5 cycles per second. That's really, really slow.

The Mind

Although the mind isn't something we can point to or describe, there are some things we can say about it. Perhaps the most important conclusion many scientists have reached in the 21st century, is that if all of the organs of the body produce the same chemicals as the brain when it's thinking, the mind comprises the entire body. *The mind's location isn't restricted to the brain; hence, the mind-body connection.*

The easiest way to understand the mind, for the sake of our discussion about hypnosis, is to think of an iceberg. Icebergs famously have about one-ninth of their mass above the surface of the water, and the rest below it. This is the perfect metaphor for your mind: only a small percentage of your thoughts and memories are in your thinking, awake state of awareness. Scientists use figures anywhere from 5-15% for the percentage of your mind that is conscious. I was taught 12% so that's what I use, plus it's pretty close to the one-ninth of the iceberg. Meanwhile, the vast majority of what you have seen, heard and experienced is below the point of consciousness. You're not able to access it any longer, under normal circumstances. You are not conscious of it; it is beneath—under—your conscious. Let's take a closer look at what occurs in your conscious and subconscious.

Your Conscious Mind

Your conscious mind has five functions.

1. Analytical
2. Rational
3. Willpower
4. Working memory
5. Voluntary body functions

HYPNOSIS MODEL

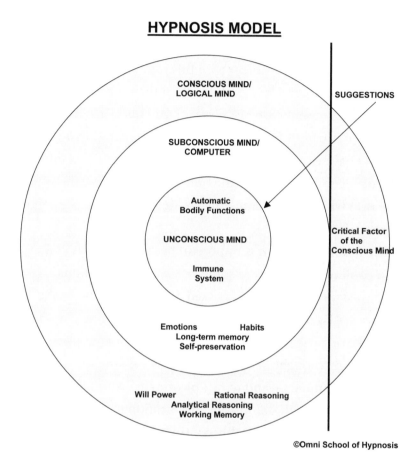

©Omni School of Hypnosis

The Critical Factor works for and protects the subconscious mind but resides in the conscious mind. Hypnosis is the by-pass of the Critical Factor of the conscious mind and the establishment of acceptable selective thinking.

1. Analytical

   Your conscious mind is logical because it is *your analytical mind.* Its job is to analyze problems and figure out how to handle them. This comes in handy when you're trying to figure out how to use the latest new technological gadget.

2. Rational

   The function of this part of your conscious mind is to give you reasons why you do the things you do. Did you ever notice that you can always come up with logical, sensible reasons for doing the things you do? We call this rationalization. The only problem with this rational reasoning is that even though it's logical, much of the time it's incorrect. This is because the true motivation for your behavior and responses comes from a deeper part of the mind that you don't have easy access to when using your conscious mind. Believe it or not, most of the time you don't know the real reason why you do something (though you will protest that you indeed do know).

The rational function is important because it allows you to conjure up answers to some very difficult questions. For instance, have you ever asked a smoker why he or she smokes? Your smoker-friend might say something like: "I smoke because it relaxes me and gives me time to pause and gather my thoughts." Even though this isn't the true reason a smoker smokes—and in fact nicotine is a stimulant and doesn't aid in relaxation—it sounds rational and logical and the smoker can comfortably continue to smoke.

In other words, the rational/rationalization function creates lies when you need them (like what your smoker-friend says). The conscious mind thinks and provides judgments, but it also protects the feelings felt by the subconscious mind, which means it will *lie* to protect the subconscious. Another example: A client says to me, "I have a great diet plan, but I eat out every night and I eat too late, so I can't stick to it." Meanwhile, the real reason for not sticking to the diet is that the subconscious wants to hold on to the weight because the client feels comfortable with her current habit pattern, which has brought her to her current weight. When she thinks about losing weight, the fear of the unknown (i.e., changing her habit pattern) arises, and she combats that fear by attributing her problem to eating out and eating late. And if that wasn't bad enough, though she continues to say she wants to "lose" weight, like most people, deep down she doesn't like the idea of "loss" or "losing." Her subconscious will help her avoid what she doesn't want: *loss*.

3. Willpower

Willpower is your ability to control your behavior by stopping and thinking about that behavior first. Willpower doesn't work very well for changing habits because it's tiring to consciously think before you act for an extended period of time. The moment you let up, the habit comes right back! All of us have tried to change something we think, do, or feel using willpower. Before coming to see me many of my clients tried to use willpower to change bad habits, such as smoking, eating poorly and not exercising, but they weren't successful. They all had the same result: temporary success, followed by a rebound right back to the habit they were trying to extinguish. And sometimes that habit was even worse after the rebound.

Willpower takes a lot of effort and you constantly have the feeling of swimming upstream because it assumes that you have something to overcome, and all that does is reinforce that you have something to overcome. You'll see later that when you use your imagination you have the opposite feeling: one of freedom and liberation.

4. Working Memory

The working memory is like a temporary workspace where you take in and work with information. Once a bit of information no longer serves a useful purpose, it seems to disappear and we seem to forget it. And unless that information is used frequently, it won't be integrated with information in the long-term memory. In other words, it will indeed disappear, which is the way it should be. We shouldn't have to remember everything we've experienced, all of the time. That would clutter up our minds too much.

5. Voluntary Body Functions

    You can stand when you want to, sit when you want to and raise your hand when you want to because your conscious mind is able to send messages to what we call your *outer shell*. Your outer shell is composed of the large muscles controlled by the conscious mind. The inner core of your body is the purview of the subconscious mind and includes functions such as: breathing, heart rate, new cell growth, and digestion. This distinction is important because if I asked you to control your digestion, could you do it? I submit that you could, but only by accessing your subconscious through some form of hypnosis.

    Notice that all of the above take some kind of effort, or work, in order to succeed at them or do them well. Oddly enough, all that energy that the conscious mind needs accounts for only 12% of your entire mind. If you're thinking that the really important stuff happens elsewhere, you're right. The really important stuff, which takes no conscious energy or effort, takes place in your subconscious mind.

Your Subconscious Mind

The subconscious mind is a level of awareness you generally don't have easy access to in a waking state, yet it represents a whopping

88% of your consciousness. Your subconscious has some features that might surprise you.

It Keeps You Alive

The subconscious doesn't think; it reacts to keep you alive. It simply, immediately does what is necessary for the benefit of your survival. And it does it quietly. It goes about its business performing all its functions and most people go through their entire lives not even knowing it exists.

Anytime the human body is traumatized, the power within is revealed. We've all heard stories like the one about the car that fell on a teenager while he was underneath it trying to fix it, and his 100-pound mother lifted the car several feet off the ground while he rolled to safety. Where did she get the power and energy for such a seemingly Herculean feat? The subconscious, which can control any part of the body if it needs to.

It's important to note that the subconscious mind protects you against danger, *both real and imagined.* The subconscious mind uses fear and anxiety to try to protect you from what it believes to be dangerous. For example, if a car veers in front of you, your subconscious fears for its life and will leap into action and command you to swerve to avoid the car. That reflex, in addition to the adrenalin that courses through you and that odd, fluttering feeling that instantly materializes in your stomach, comes from your subconscious. However, your subconscious might also protect you against spiders, which you for some reason imagine might be harmful to you so they cause you anxiety. That's how phobias develop. The subconscious is just trying to protect you; it doesn't think and therefore it has no idea that there's nothing it needs to protect you from in reality. The subconscious protects you against both real and imagined dangers because . . .

It houses your imagination and it cannot differentiate between what is real and what is imagined.

All of us were born with a marvelous faculty we call imagination. It seems like every child has more than his share. Nevertheless, almost immediately, teachers, parents and other well-meaning adults attempt to turn it off. We must learn to deal with—and in—"reality," they say. To many people, however, "reality" means worrying, anxiety, hard work and no fun. And to those people I say: What if everyone in the world turned off his imagination? We would never have anything new. As you may know, Thomas Edison failed 3,000 times when working on the light bulb. He had every reason to give up. In his biography, he talks about how much fodder for his continued experimentation arose out of catnaps. The images during his catnaps were the tools his subconscious mind used to explore, communicate and hypothesize. Scientists who study inventors know that many of their most creative ideas come when they're off doing something other than focusing on a problem; when they're minds are free to imagine.

The subconscious mind records everything you experience, real and imaginary, as a memory, and reacts to both with the same intensity. Hypnosis uses this concept to help you reprogram your behavior. Many hypnosis techniques use the imagination to help you actually change what your subconscious is thinking and feeling.

(Note that because of the subjective nature of long-term memory, we never assume that a memory recalled in hypnosis was something that actually happened. We may address it in hypnosis *as if* it really happened, but we would never assume that it had.)

It's important to know that in the same way the imagination can help you reach your goals, it can prevent you from reaching them. Many of the difficulties you experience in your life probably originate in your imagination. And they are so powerful that your mind transforms them into reality. Once again, your 88% overrides your 12%.

The best way to demonstrate that your subconscious mind can't differentiate between what is real and what is imagined is what I call The Lemon Test. Read the following a couple of times until you have committed the short process to memory. Then, close your eyes and see what happens!

Imagine you are in your kitchen on a bright sunny day. Look around you and notice the colors and the light in the room.

Slowly work your way to the refrigerator, noticing everything along the way. Notice which way the door to the refrigerator opens. When you open the door you notice a lemon on the shelf in front of you. Look at a lemon. Feel it. Pick it up, bring it to a cutting board next to the sink, and pick up the sharp knife lying next to the cutting board. Slice the bright, yellow lemon in half. Imagine yourself smelling the lemon, bringing it to your mouth, and then squeezing some of the juice onto your tongue.

Did you salivate? Did your mouth pucker? Did you notice a taste that reminded you of something? Through your thoughts about the lemon, you created a physical reaction. Isn't it amazing how easy it is? *Thoughts can create physical reactions.* Your imagination created a physical reaction.

Finally, and I'll repeat this later, when you use your imagination, you don't want to get bogged down in the minutiae of how you'll get to your destination. *Why?* Because there are many ways to get there. To assume that you know the best way, and to concentrate on that best way, could, in the end, derail you and prevent you from getting what you want. In fact, to assume there is a best way is to essentially *not* use your imagination at all! File away your problem-solving skills and your willpower and simply imagine yourself possessing vitality, focus and the ability to perform flawlessly in whatever sport you're involved in. Imagine yourself at your best and let your subconscious figure out the most effective way to make your best happen for you. Imagine your problems solved.

Your Subconscious Mind Can't Think, Reason or Argue

And it can't judge the merit of an idea, either. But it *can* do something very powerful: it can tell you whether something is smooth or rough, hot or cold, sad or funny, and painful or pleasurable. It feels.

It's Your Emotional Mind

You have feelings about everything in your life, but most of the time they are beneath your conscious awareness. Ordinarily, when something triggers an emotion, the subconscious opens so you can experience that emotion consciously. Whether you do in fact have a conscious experience, or whether you have learned to keep your emotions out of your conscious awareness, they still exist. They live in your subconscious. So if you need to change them (like when maybe they're running your life) you now know where to find them.

Your Subconscious=You

Who you are, how you respond, and what you believe, are functions of your subconscious mind. All of your automatic responses come from your subconscious mind, including your beliefs. You don't have to stop to figure out what you believe to be true in order to respond to a situation. You simply know what you believe, and your responses are based on your beliefs.

Everything about you is stored in your subconscious. Your

experiences, thoughts, fantasies, daydreams and night dreams. This occurs because, again, your subconscious mind cannot tell the difference between something that's actually happening to you and something that you're imagining.

Your Habits Are a Function of Your Subconscious

This is part of *Your Subconscious-You* but deserves a section of its own. When you do the same thing in the same way, with enough repetition the subconscious mind will make it a habit. That's why when we speak of habits we say we're doing things "without thinking." A habit is an automatic response, or reminder to respond, to a certain situation in a specific way. Much of what you do every day is by habit. For example, when you get up in the morning and leave the house, at some point you get dressed, right? You don't leave the house and go out in public naked, do you? Have you ever? Why not? Because you have developed a habit pattern, starting when you were a toddler, that when you leave the house you must wear clothing. You don't even think about it. In fact, it's such an odd thing to pay attention to, isn't it? That's what happens when you analyze something the subconscious does: it becomes alien to you because you're used to seeing only the result, and not what happens behind the scenes.

Our subconscious has developed habit patterns that help us and haunt us. For instance, we learn that we need to stop at a red light long before we learn how to drive. Being in cars with parents and friends during our childhood and adolescence sends us messages about what you do and don't do when you drive. When the time finally comes when you get behind the wheel and drive off by yourself, you don't give a moment's thought to a red light; you merely slow to a stop. And that habit, whether or not you think of it this way, saves your life.

As for habits that haunt us, I think of people who insist on referring to themselves as "social smokers." They find themselves subconsciously picking up a cigarette when they order a drink or walk into a bar. They've convinced themselves that alcohol and cigarettes "go together," and that "it's natural" to have a drink in one hand and a "butt" in the other. And their subconscious minds must corroborate that idea by creating the behavior to support it. *They become what they think.* Luckily, any habit can be changed by working with the subconscious mind through hypnosis. Even the habit of calling yourself a social smoker and the habit of smoking. Fortunately, it's never too late, and you're never too old, to change your habits. You can begin today. You can begin right now, at this very moment.

Habits don't go away, but they can be replaced if you work at it. Fortunately, we now know how habits are created and where they live in your brain (in the basal ganglia, if you must know). Again, when we say that habits are things we do "without thinking," that's actually literally correct. Habits emerge as a way to save effort, which is one of the characteristics of the brain; it wants to exert as little energy as possible by making behaviors automatic.

If you could change by just reading a book about change or going to therapy or hearing a fantastic argument about why you needed to change, everyone would be replacing all of their negative thoughts and behaviors with positive ones. But it's not that easy. Reading doesn't create change easily or automatically. Logic doesn't create change. You need something more.

One of the things you need to do to change a behavior is repetition. You need practice. What you use increases, and what you don't use will atrophy from lack of use. All of your healthy habits increase or decrease in proportion to the extent to which you apply them. Once a habit is formed, it becomes easier and easier to follow and more difficult to replace.

It makes sense, then, that a surefire way to tell what your future will hold is to look at your habits of today. If you don't change any of your habits of today, there's one place they'll inevitably lead you.

How the Conscious and the Subconscious Work Together

The subconscious and the conscious minds complement each other; they work together, each doing separate tasks. The simplest (though imperfect) metaphor to use is that of the computer. The conscious mind is like the desktop on the display. Imagine the desktop: what's there? The icons for files you're dealing with right now, and the ones you can easily access with the click of a mouse. Meanwhile, your subconscious mind is like hard drive that stores all of your files and programs. It warehouses everything, plus it's responsible for everything working smoothly.

Regardless of whether you believe your hard drive was empty when you were born or was already filled with thoughts and memories from lives past, it can still be reprogrammed. Little by little, your hard drive has been programmed by your life experience so that today you are a sum total of everything that has ever happened to you. Every day, your subconscious mind gets visual input, auditory input and tactile input totaling 150,000 to 300,000 words and images. Every day. Everything. Impressions of everything you've ever done, seen, heard, tasted, smelled, or imagined, are all stored somewhere in your subconscious mind. Even images from your peripheral vision—images that you didn't even focus on—have been cataloged and stored in your subconscious.

Everything? Yes, because your subconscious holds your long-term memory (sometimes called permanent memory). Recall that I mentioned that you seem to have forgotten some things from your past. The important word there is *seem.* In reality, you haven't forgotten anything that has happened to you. Every impression is stored somewhere in your subconscious mind. Using certain hypnotherapy techniques, you can recall or re-experience early childhood events, even as far back as your birth experience.

With hypnosis, you can also change your attitudes and beliefs and thereby change your emotional responses. It's possible to reduce guilt, anger, hatred and resentment, opening you up to experience more emotions such as care, joy and happiness. Who wouldn't want more of those?

You can even strengthen your memory, as deep relaxation brings harmony and close rapport between your conscious and subconscious and makes it easier for them to cooperate. In a state of hypnosis, they work together swimmingly and seamlessly.

If you're still unclear about how your conscious and subconscious minds work together, try this clarifying exercise . . .

As you retire for the night, make yourself as comfortable as possible. Close your eyes and relax. Ask yourself a question to which you've temporarily forgotten the answer. It can pertain to anything:

- the name of an old friend
- a long-forgotten teacher
- an old address
- a phone number
- a word in a foreign language that you learned but cannot recall

What you're doing is using your conscious mind to locate something that isn't there; it isn't in your conscious mind. Be specific and also be sure that you once knew the information you're requesting. It has to be in there somewhere in order for you to access it. This isn't about creating, it's about locating. You're locating it *in your subconscious mind*.

Next, command that sometime the following day you'll have a revelatory thought about your question—that you will suddenly find the answer in your mind and recognize it as the answer.

Just as soon as you've asked your question and have set the state for receiving the answer, forget about it and quietly go to sleep. Your subconscious will unfailingly give you the answer to your question if you let it. The same applies for the next day: stay occupied and don't let your mind wander back on the question. And certainly don't obsess over it. Your subconscious cannot function as directed if your conscious mind is constantly interfering.

When you least expect it, the answer will appear.

Hypnosis is simply about making a change in the subconscious mind. This is very powerful because if a suggestion is allowed to go into your subconscious mind, then it has the power to change your beliefs and change your behaviors. So how does a suggestion get into your subconscious? In other words, how does hypnosis happen?

The Critical Factor of the Conscious Mind

There's another part of the mind, which operates automatically when you're using your conscious mind. Dave Elman, the Vaudevillian-turned-radio producer-turned hypnotist famous for his rapid induction technique that I mentioned earlier, called it *the critical factor of the conscious mind* and it acts as a filter or critic or judge of all suggestions presented to you. Its job is to protest the status quo of your beliefs in your subconscious mind. This is an important function because if you didn't have it, anyone could walk up to you and say something to manipulate you. When you hear a suggestion, your critical factor checks with your subconscious mind to see if that suggestion is in agreement with your existing beliefs. If it is, the suggestion is allowed to go into your subconscious and the belief is made stronger. If it isn't, the suggestion is rejected and there's no change.

You can see the critical factor in action when you try to discuss religion or politics with someone who has different beliefs than you. Because the critical factor doesn't allow the opposing belief to enter the subconscious, you keep steadfast to your own thoughts. So how do we get suggestions into that subconscious mind? How can we effect change of belief and habits? We use hypnosis.

According to Elman, hypnosis bypasses the critical factor of the conscious mind in order to open the door to your subconscious mind (i.e., your hard drive) and focus the mind to accept positive information, such as encouraging suggestions. In other words, a hypnotist is a kind of human computer re-programmer. If an idea is permitted to enter into your subconscious, you are positioned to change. In fact, you will automatically begin to respond differently.

In hypnosis, we push the conscious mind aside. We open the door to the subconscious mind, enter it, and that's where we work. Adults have a very hardcore critical factor made up of all the facts and figures and nonsense they've picked up through the years. This critical factor will leap to the defense of any preconditioned idea and instantly refute it.

Note that belief, which is an important subconscious mechanism, is necessary in order to create and sustain change. You must believe it is possible (more on this in a moment).

I mention Dave Elman and his critical factor of the conscious mind because I think his was a great, simple way to describe how hypnosis works. But the reality—the science—says that we're not sure why it works. We don't doubt it does work, but at this point in neuroscience we haven't yet mapped out the precise *way* that it works. And that's probably because what we are calling the subconscious mind isn't located in one, or even two specific places. Instead, it's a characteristic of various parts of the brain, some of which is responsible for both conscious and subconscious behavior.

Why a hypnotist can't control you . . .

If hypnosis were just about bypassing the critical factor, we hypnotists would be able to control our clients. All hypnotists would be billionaires, we'd have flawless tennis games and golf rounds, and we'd all be thin, for sure. But since we know that's not the case, I want to address the one element to hypnosis that prevents a hypnotist from being able to control you: you never lose the awareness of the suggestions give to you.

Yes, when you enter hypnosis the critical factor is bypassed, but now your conscious mind takes on the important job of protecting you against suggestions that aren't good for you or that you don't whole-heartedly want. You see, when you're in hypnosis, you can hear perfectly everything that's going on. Actually, all of your five senses become sharper and more powerful. Your state of awareness is heightened and your ability to decide what you will and won't do, or what you will or won't accept, is much stronger when you're in hypnosis. Your conscious mind is still aware and you can hear every suggestion that is given to you.

You've Been Hypnotized Thousands of Times

A hypnotic state (also called a trance) is a natural state of mind. You go in and out of hypnotic trances all day long; you'd be surprised how many times your critical factor is being bypassed every day. For example, we've all heard of highway hypnosis. That's when you're driving down the road and you don't remember driving the last block or maybe the last several miles or perhaps you missed your turn. That's because while you were daydreaming, your subconscious mind took over driving for your own protection.

We tend to zone out and get very relaxed while watching television, one of the great hypnotizers. Sometimes we even ignore things going on around us when watching television. Add to that the fact that advertisers know everything hypnotists know about bypassing your critical factor. Advertisers use that knowledge to suggest to you or to hypnotize you into buying their products. Branding experts, in particular, use the principles of hypnosis to persuade you that you simply must acquire *the feeling* that the brand will give you: that you must buy their products because you can't be happy or whole without them. Think of how mindlessly you walk through a department store, directly to the brand—the designer—whose clothes you ordinarily buy. Why?

Authority figures can also bypass your critical factors. For example, you'll tend to believe people you look up to: those whom you think know more than you do. This includes doctors, schoolteachers, preachers and motivational speakers. All kinds of people bypass your critical factor. Any time you're feeling a strong emotion such as love or fear, anger or grief, you're more suggestible. Things said to you, or things you say to yourself, will bypass your critical factor and become part of your subconscious programming. In other words, you don't have to be in any kind of relaxed state at all to accept suggestion. You don't even need to close your eyes. We call this waking hypnosis, and it happens every day.

Hypnosis Can Extinguish Fears and Phobias

Phobias, extreme anxiety, some fears and excessive behaviors can all be extinguished through hypnosis, although they require more than just the average positive suggestion to impact them significantly (I use hypnosis in addition to Neuro-Linguistic Programming for phobias, with great success). We don't develop phobias out of a habit, but rather because of some situation that profoundly frightened us in the past. Usually, this situation occurred during early childhood, yet we continue to relive it—and even exaggerate it. For example, most people have fear of public speaking to some degree and many people are terrified of snakes, spiders, flying, or heights. We learn these fears from early experiences, sometimes long forgotten. With hypnotherapy techniques, you can remove your fear by changing the response where it lives: in the subconscious mind.

But you have to have the right attitude . . .

Attitude is Everything

The mental attitude you hold when you hear a suggestion determines whether it goes into your internal computer in order for change to begin, or whether it's rejected and there will be no change. Three attitudes affect your hypnotic state:

1. When you hear a suggestion, your attitude is: "Boy I like that suggestion. I know that it's going to work beautifully for me!" And it will. This attitude means that you passionately want and trust the suggestion, and it should be allowed into your subconscious mind. And because the suggestion is allowed to go into your subconscious, the change happens.

2. When you hear a suggestion, you're thinking: "I don't know, there's just something a little uncomfortable about that

suggestion." With this attitude, you'll reject the suggestion
and there won't be any change in your subconscious.

3. When you hear a suggestion, you're neutral. For example,
    you don't care if you get it or you don't get it, but you're
    willing to try new things. Unfortunately, there's not enough
    energy behind that suggestion for it to make much of an
    impression, so it's rejected and there's no change. If you've
    ever heard someone say something like, "I tried hypnosis
    and it didn't work," that's because, providing they had
    some sessions in the first place, they probably held on
    to this last mental attitude and caused their own failure.
    When they heard a suggestion they said to themselves, "I
    like that suggestion. I sure hope it works." What they didn't
    realize was that hope means doubt, and doubt rejects the
    suggestion.

You can hope all day long that I'm going to make you change,
and it simply won't happen. I cannot control you. But if you want
the change and you focus on the suggestion with a positive attitude,
trusting that it will work, the suggestion will be allowed in and positive change will happen!

Let's take your good attitude through a discussion about NLP . . .

CHAPTER 2

WHAT IS NEURO-LINGUISTIC PROGRAMMING, AND WHY DO I USE IT?

NEURO-LINGUISTIC Programming (NLP) is used by millions of people around the world in a variety of fields, including: sports, business, education, therapy and personal development. Though there isn't one, definitive version of the history of NLP that all of the parties involved agree on, everyone does agree that two twenty-somethings at the University of California at Santa Cruz started NLP in the early 1970s. Richard Bandler, a psychology student, and John Grinder, an associate professor of linguistics, began studying the thinking and behavioral skills used by particularly effective and successful people.

Two of the successful people Bandler and Grinder studied were Virginia Satir (who's considered the mother of Family Therapy) and Fritz Perls (the founder of Gestalt Therapy). They were able to extract the thoughts and behaviors that they felt were largely responsible for the success of Satir, Perls, and the others they studied, and they presented their findings in workshops.

Bandler and Grinder were introduced to the work of Milton Erickson and began pondering hypnotic techniques in addition to their growing (and by then diverse) body of knowledge about effectiveness and success that they called NLP. Their initial target audience was therapists and they published books, facilitated seminars and workshops, and produced a cadre of students, some of whom went on to start their own NLP centers.

By the early 1980s, Bandler and Grinder went their separate ways. But NLP kept growing and diversifying, with an increasingly strong presence in England. It was officially becoming a movement.

What exactly is NLP?

NLP has been called an owner's manual for your brain. It has also been called the study of excellence, the study of success and the science of achievement. And all that is accurate. NLP is a practical explanation of how to succeed in communication, relationships and life. It's based on observable phenomena, not theories, and it works. Most important, it's a simple process that at its core has two steps:

1. NLP examines success for its underlying patterns of thought, belief and behavior.
2. It seeks to reproduce the thoughts, beliefs and behaviors that create success, thereby reproducing success.

Examine success for patterns, then reproduce those patterns, thereby reproducing success.

N= Neuro, referring to the mind (and particularly its connection to the body).

L= Linguistic, referring to the potential for change using language.

P= Programming, meaning the study of patterns that create success and failure, and programming yourself with the success patterns.

When you become knowledgeable and, more important, skilled, in the techniques of NLP, you'll be able to:

- Learn new things faster than before.
- Master what you can already do well.
- Manage your emotions more effectively.
- Improve your relationships.
- Communicate more effectively.
- Think more clearly.
- Create healthier, more positive behaviors.
- Concentrate better.
- Have the courage to become who you want to be.
- Enjoy life more than ever before.

Getting Started

If you want to produce any kind of lasting change in your behavior, including improvement in your athletic performance, the decision to change is your first step. Then comes learning whatever it is you need to learn to create your change. The final part, which is probably most important, is practice.

I constantly hear people saying things like, "I'm going to take my game to a whole different level this year" or "This is the year I'm going to overcome my fear of hitting the ball into the net." What keeps many people from accomplishing these types of goals is simple: we get attached to our past because it's made of what we practiced most.

The bottom line is that the past creates the future. And if you want to change, remaining attached to past experiences solves nothing and serves only to create an environment where healing is impossible, and reproduction of the past is inevitable. You create a vicious cycle where negative experiences and negative images are reinforced, which leads to more negative outcomes. As they say, the definition of insanity is *doing the same thing over and over and expecting a different result.*

Neuro-Linguistic Programming is a great way to create changes in your ability to move through your athletic performance, but if you want to accelerate your progress, I believe you need to use NLP in conjunction with hypnosis. There's simply nothing more powerful than enlisting the subconscious when you desire change.

NLP Essentials

NLP techniques set out to alter our verbal and nonverbal communication so we produce the results and reactions we intend to produce. There are plenty of books on NLP in your local library and your local bookstore, and there are several websites dedicated to it. And while there are some subtle and not-so-subtle differences in interpretations of NLP and its use, there are also some essentials that everyone agrees on. Here's a set of essential principles of NLP, which we call *presuppositions.* No matter who you are, how much money you have, how much you weigh, how long you've been unhappy, or how fast you can run a mile, these will be true for you.

- **There is no such thing as failure. There is only feedback.**
  If you're regularly successful at anything, chances are you have developed patterns of thoughts, feelings and actions that have left little room for any other outcome. With a few exceptions, there are no flukes when it comes to outcome. Every outcome, whether you view it as a failure or a success, is really just an outcome. And every outcome has a clear path that leads to it.
  We're all products of patterns that we have

created—consciously and subconsciously—for our entire lives. Two things about us are because of chance: genetics (the biology we were born with which is internal) and occurrences outside us over which we have no control, such as plane crashes and other accidents. The rest of how our physical being came to be what it is because of what we have ingested, the environment we live in and how we behave. This can be good, as we may have developed patterns that serve us—that work for us. But it can also be bad, as we have unwittingly developed patterns that are destructive, or at best unproductive.

Your physical tennis game, your golf game, your triathlon performance, and the way you pitch a ball all come from habit patterns you've created. And if the results you've been getting aren't what you want, you need to change your habit patterns. According to NLP there is no such thing as failure; there is only feedback. And if the feedback you have isn't what you want, you should change whatever you can change: what you eat/your environment/how you sleep/how you exercise/how you think in order to change the feedback. If you want new results, change yourself. Change the input that creates the output.

Going back to the core of NLP, you can change yourself by creating a list of behaviors that work and don't work in your life (that's the *examine success* part I referred to earlier). Work backwards from your successes and your failures, and list what you did that caused the outcome. There's no judgment about good and bad; there's simply what works and what doesn't work.

- **Everything that happens is neutral.**
  Similar to the above presupposition, simply put on a
  bumper sticker I recently saw: "Life happens." In reality,
  everything that happens is neutral. Life, death, accidents;
  they're all neutral. And we can leave them neutral, or we
  can decide to label them positive or negative, thereby giving
  them a life they didn't have when they were merely neutral.
  The way you look at life can affect the body and how it
  performs, and that includes your athletic performance.
  Fortunately, we all have the innate ability to choose how we
  look at any given set of circumstances or events. In NLP, we
  refer to "reframing" as that shifting of our perspective, and
  in turn changing our approach and probably changing the
  outcome.

- **The meaning of a communication is the response you get.**
  One of the areas compromised by performance anxiety and
  the frustration that accompanies it is communication. Many
  people find that when their athletic performance is suffering
  or not optimal, that dissatisfaction bleeds into other areas.
  For example, their relationships aren't going as smoothly
  and their miscommunications and disagreements increase.
  Though getting defensive and blaming other people is an
  understandable reaction, remember that although you
  always have an intention behind your communications,
  those intentions are meaningless unless they match the
  messages that those around you receive. If someone receives
  a message that doesn't match your intention, the responsibility falls on you to change that outcome. As we say in NLP,
  you may not be getting the response you want, but you'll
  always get a response to what the other person heard.

- **The map is not the territory.**

  NLP is about altering your perceptions, as they are what define what you call "reality." Your memory, for example, is not an exact replication of what has occurred in your life. However, it defines your reality. So you have this map in your head regarding your history and experiences and abilities, and obviously it hasn't served you perfectly because you're now trying to improve your athletic performance. But the point is that just because you have a map, doesn't mean it represents the territory. Though your map was true for the past (as it landed you here), it isn't necessarily true for the present territory you're in. But your brain will continue to use the map again and again, unless and until you tell it not to and you present it with a more powerful map that you regularly use. There's a high probability that the maps you're using regarding your athletic performance don't correspond to the territory you're navigating, yet you use them anyway, and (of course) they steer you back to the old destination.

- **You cannot not communicate.**

  Think about it. Everything someone else can see, hear or feel, that is coming from you, is communicating something about what you are thinking and feeling. Your body language, eye movement, and tone of voice all send a message, as do the speed of your breath and the pace of your speech. We all communicate virtually all the time—we can't help it. When you walk up to a starting line or a golf tee, *without saying a word*, what are *you* communicating to your opponents and anyone else present?

  Some of the things that come from you that might then

affect others are in your control, and others don't appear to be. Emotions, for instance, begin internally. Then they produce physiological changes that occur in your body that tend to produce predictable outer manifestations. And those outer manifestations might affect others. Here are a few examples of this phenomenon.

Anger

When you're angry your heart and breathing rates jump, your blood flows to your hands in preparation to hit something, and your overall energy increases. The volume and projection of your voice also increase, in order to attempt to instill fear in anyone who is threatening to you.

When George gets angry about another bad serve, he says out loud, "I am the worst player on the planet!" And then sometimes he smashes his racket on the ground in disappointment. Not only has he told his mind, not to mention the rest of the world, that he isn't a good player, but he's tearing up the court while risking the cost and inconvenience of broken equipment. In addition, those observing him won't have a positive impression of him, which can affect other things, such as not getting invited out to play again or limiting his ability to get new clients.

Fear

When you're in fear, your heart and breathing speed up, but your blood takes a different direction: it leaves your face and surges to your legs for a quick escape (the flight portion of fight of flight—see above for the fight part). Momentarily, your body freezes, making it possible to determine if hiding would be better than running. The volume and projection of your voice lessen to minimize the potential of drawing attention.

Disgust

Disgust is usually indicated by the shunning of your sense. For instance, your eyes squint, your face turns away, your lips curl, and your nose wrinkles. Your vocalization becomes staccato and is marked by quick, short outburst of breath, similar to what you do when you spit out unwanted food.

Love

Love is a relaxed state marked by increasing blood flow to the lips and hands accompanied by an open physical bearing and deep breathing, which facilitate contentment and cooperation. Vocalization becomes more resonant, perhaps to soothe and charm.

- **What you think is what you get.**
  I've found that there are four mental-conditioning principles for the conscious mind that are particularly helpful to my clients:

    1. You are what you concentrate on.
    2. What you concentrate on seems real (because real and imagined cannot be differentiated).
    3. What you concentrate on grows.
    4. You always find what you concentrate on.

- **You don't know what you don't know.**
  In NLP's model of learning, we call this unconscious incompetence. Experts/coaches/therapists/hypnotherapists are

helpful because you don't know what you don't know. But
once you do, you are at the point of choice. Then, you know
what you don't know, and you can choose to do something
about it.

In NLP, when we achieve excellence, we say that we have
evolved from . . .

**unconscious incompetence → conscious incompetence →
conscious competence → unconscious competence**

Think of it this way: unconscious incompetence is how
you start to play any sport. You don't know what you don't
know. Then you learn about just how much you don't know;
you reach a state of conscious incompetence.

After some lessons and practicing, you become aware of
what you're doing that's resulting in success; you reach a
state of conscious competence. And finally, you reach a state
where you're no longer aware of thinking about what you
are doing to achieve success. This is your ultimate goal, and
it is called unconscious competence.

- **If one person can learn to do something, so can you.**
  This doesn't mean that you can play like Tiger Woods just
  because you're both humans who know how to play golf.
  But it does mean that you can learn from his success. There's
  always something we can learn from the success of others.
  We might not be physically able to duplicate what they do,
  but that doesn't mean we can't improve what *we're* doing.
  The fastest way toward excellence is to find someone who
  already exhibits it and do what they do. NLP uses several

techniques to produce and reproduce excellence. The ones I use most in my practice are:

- Modeling
- Circle of Excellence
- Theatre of the Mind
- Anchoring

Modeling

The theory of Modeling says that we can achieve excellence in anything by finding a place where it already exists and copying the traits and behaviors present when excellence is present. Everyone needs a role model, and this takes the use of the role model a step further in that you'll actually *model the behavior of the role model.*

- Imagine someone playing (or running or skating) with ease, poise and confidence. They are balanced. Keep that image in your mind for a moment.
- Look at the person's body, from the tips of their feet to the top of their head. Memorize the person. Put yourself in their position.
- What are you thinking about that allows you to be in that position? What are you feeling?

These are the thoughts and feelings you want to develop. This is modeling.

Meanwhile, back in your real life…

When you're on the court or in the rink, what do you ordinarily think about? What do you feel? What ordinarily occurs during your competitive athletic performances?

- Are you thinking about work?
- Are you thinking about the last conversation you had with your spouse?
- Are you thinking about your weight?
- Are you thinking about your financial situation?

And when you're thinking about all of these things, are you focused on the negative? If so, you shouldn't be surprised when your performance isn't spectacular. What you think is what you get. If your mind isn't in a space of peak performance, your body won't be, either.

Circle of Excellence

The **Circle of Excellence** is the people and images, sights and sounds, you surround yourself with that are indicative of excellence, and that exude excellence.

Picture yourself in the middle of a circle, and then fill that circle with whatever has contributed to your excellence and whatever is proof of your excellence. Accessing that mental image—and its corresponding confidence and self-esteem—recreates that excellence. Remember, the subconscious mind responds as if that circle is your reality.

Note that when NLP refers to excellence and what has caused it, it's referring to what we can directly observe as the cause of excellence. This isn't about theorizing about what actions *might* have resulted in or contributed to a state of excellence. This is about cause and effect. What people, actions, places, and processes have contributed to your success? Visualize them and place them in your circle.

Theater of the Mind

If you're thinking that Theatre of the Mind is characterized by visualization, you're correct. The better you are at using your imagination, the more successful you'll be when you use Theater of the Mind later. Here's how it works:

- Make a movie of yourself in the outcome you want, such as running a flawless marathon and winning. You're the director and you're also the star. Create the entire scene. What do you look like? Who's around you? What's around you? What kind of day is it? What are you wearing? What's on your feet? The objective is to create as realistic a vision as possible of the outcome you'd like to achieve.
- Add as much sensory information as you can pack into your movie. It's 3-D, it's scratch and sniff, and you can even taste it. Remember to also add internal dialogue. In movies, there are voiceovers to tell us what the characters are thinking. What are you thinking? What are you feeling? How would you describe your inner life? What is the sports commentator saying as you run the marathon?

Here are some tips for effective Theater of the Mind experiences:

- Learn to control your imagination. Practice visualizing. Imagine that your hands are lighter and lighter and your feet are heavier and heavier. It might sounds like hocus pocus, but if you can master these exercises, you can affect your body with your mind. That skill is highly desirable—in fact vital—to success using Theater of the Mind and hypnosis.
- Learn to use your imagination when preparing for your

events or games. Pay close attention to everything around you. Attend to things you usually take for granted, like your gait, your posture and your hair. Though these details may seem like minutiae, they'll be helpful later when you're creating one of your Theater of the Mind productions.

- Develop your creativity. Visualize new inventions, new services, new movies, and new approaches to athletic performance. Imagination and creativity are more popular than ever at your local bookstore. Scientists have been studying them and journalists and experts have written some entertaining and enlightening books on them in the past few years. Want insight into how to improve your creativity? You just might find it in a book!
- When your perception tells you you're up against a wall, let your imagination run wild. Brainstorm. Don't judge your ideas or edit them—just let them flow and associate freely. Don't focus too much, as focus is an obstacle to creativity.
- Practice and practice and practice until you are comfortable using your imagination easily and effectively.

Anchoring

Anchoring is a technique that creates a response through the use of association. It's based on classical behavioral conditioning and involves creating a trigger that will be connected to a desired response. It completely bypasses your conscious and creates and instant reaction; the conscious mind can't stop the reaction you have programmed. If you're familiar with the language of the habit loop (cue leads to behavior that leads to reward), the trigger or anchor is the cue. The cue/anchor/trigger might be something that already causes a reaction or behavior. What we're going to do is change the association you have. We're replacing your old reaction (habit) with a new one.

Anchors can be just about anything: a touch (e.g., taking the racket); a sight (e.g., seeing the course you're about to play); or a complex set of movements (e.g., when you approach the starting line). The important part is to attach the anchor to a desired emotional response. For example: *When you take the racket, you immediately relax.* I've found that anchoring is the tool that creates the most powerful, lasting changes in my clients. I use it multiple times in all of my personal sessions and all of my CDs, and I recommend that you get comfortable with it and use it when you create self-hypnosis scripts of your own. You can try to use anchoring on the conscious level to replace a reaction or habit you have with a different one, but as I discussed at the beginning of this section, in my experience accessing the subconscious is the quicker, easier way to go. And it's far less exhausting because it doesn't involve willpower!

Final Thoughts on NLP
Controlling Your Internal and External Dialogue

You are the only person who can, within a moment of thinking or saying something, stop that thought. You are at the control panel of your thinking. Here are a few ways you can change your thinking, *real time.*

Cancel. The moment you catch yourself saying something negative, say, "cancel," out loud, and replace the thought with
something positive. If you have difficulty coming up with a
replacement, override your negative thought or word with
the image of a purple elephant. *Why?* Because there's no
such thing as a purple elephant; it doesn't exist. Therefore,

you couldn't have developed any kind of negative association with it. It merely takes up some space for a moment,
and you move on. Cancel works well for don't, not, and
woulda/coulda/shoulda, as well.

Snap It! Put a rubber band around your wrist. The moment you
have a negative thought or speak a negative word, snap it.
This provides you with an uncomfortable feeling that you
then associate your negative talk. In short order, you will
condition yourself to avoid the bad feeling or the snap, by
way of stopping what creates it (your negative self-talk).

Easy. There are many aspects of every sport that work well with
the idea of "Easy," which is just like "Cancel," and you can
try them now, on the conscious level, or create a script for
yourself for self-hypnosis. Let's say you have difficulty with
your serve. You can program yourself to immediately think
of the word—see the word—"Easy" when you approach the
line. It's a form of anchoring where you take an existing cue
and tack an "Easy" onto it and *presto*, you replace whatever
you used to experience with instant ease and relaxation.

CHAPTER 3

THE LAWS OF THE UNIVERSE AND THE NATURAL LAWS OF THE MIND

THE following laws came to me by way the amazing Dorothy Gates, Ph.D. whom I introduced in Chapter One. She was my mentor and my friend, and she saved my life. You'll find that the laws have a lot in common with philosophical and spiritual traditions that originated in the East and have been increasingly accepted in the West. Some of them were introduced in the United States during the New Age movement and were dismissed as "fluff," but since then plenty of evidence has been amassed that they're valid and not as whimsical, nonscientific, and "out there" as they once considered.

The Laws of the Universe

The Laws of the Universe are exactly what they sound like: they describe the way the universe--the energy of the universe--functions. Because they are laws, they are always true.

THE LAW OF ATTRACTION

We attract to us what we project out into the world through our thoughts, feelings, and actions. Like magnets, we send a powerful message about what we want, and we get it. The only problem is that most of us don't realize that's what we're doing.

Thoughts are energy, feelings are energy, and actions are energy, and *like attracts like,* meaning energy gravitates toward energy that is similar to it. Everyone's thoughts, feelings and actions, combined, in addition to everything that surrounds us, is the central engine of our being and our consciousness as a species. We are all part of the same energy field. It influences us, and we influence it in return. All things that are alike gather together; they attract each other. So if you are positive, you gather with other positive energies; you attract them. And if you are negative, you attract other negative energies. *What do you want to attract?* Whatever it is, begin by projecting it.

THE LAW OF CAUSE AND EFFECT

There can be no effect without a cause. Think about it. Things don't just happen--they're the results of your thoughts, actions and deeds. And in terms of your mind, as we saw in Chapter One, that means that your results are the 12%, but the causes can be found in the 88% of your mind. Therefore, though everything has a cause, it's likely that you might not know what that cause is. You need to tap into your huge 88% in order to create real, sustained change.

My Favorite Dorothy Gates-isms

Dorothy had dozens of great one-, two-, and even three-liners, based on basic laws of the universe. Some of my favorites are:

- Every action must be followed by an appropriate reaction. There's no exception of any kind, at any time, for any reason.
- There can be no effect without a cause. (Think about it.

Things don't just happen—they're the results thoughts, actions or genetics. In terms of your mind, that means that your results are the 12% that is your conscious mind, but the cause can be found in the 88% of your mind that is subconscious. Therefore, though everything has a cause, it's likely that you might not know what cause it is. You need to tap into your huge 88% in order to create real, sustained change.)

- We get out of life what we put into life—no more and no less.

- If we make mistakes in life, we eventually pay the price. We are largely the creators of our own destiny.

- Thoughts we dwell upon in our minds are the seeds, and the seeds will create an entire harvest according to the law of 'like produces like.' All seeds must reproduce according to type. Seed determines the type, harvest reveals the seed sown.

- Having an *attitude of gratitude* is part of creating your future, as you'll attract more of what you tell the universe you are grateful for. Sporadic moments of gratitude aren't enough; you must make a habit of continuously expressing and projecting how thankful you are.

Thanks to Dorothy, I have learned to use my energy to attract and create what I need for my own personal happiness and balance, and to her, I am eternally grateful.

THE LAW OF FREE THOUGHT

We can choose to use our free thought and free will for good or not, and we'll always face the consequences of our choices—sooner or later. We are the sum total of our choices.

Peace, plenty and security aren't detached from us; they aren't things that exist apart from us. In fact, they are inside of us, and if we choose to think and believe that's true, it will be true.

THE LAW OF WORK

We live in two spheres: vocational and personal. The wise person seeks to achieve harmony between the two. Our purpose is to make a contribution while we're here, and to advance the act of living to some degree by having lived. We should all be occupied in the highest employment our nature is capable of, and leave this lifetime with the consciousness that we've done our best. No one can ask more of you than that you do your best.

THE LAW OF HUMAN RELATIONS

Society is an extension of the individual. The first human unit is the individual, then the family, the community, the city, the nation, and the world. The contribution of every nation is the result of the quality of its citizens. So if you think your community, your state, or your nation needs improvement, you can be the starting point of that improvement. And in case you're thinking someone else will be the starting point, what if they're thinking that, too?

We owe it to ourselves and to each other to do what we can to promote peace and compassion. Remember that one warped mind affects everyone in the community. We've seen that time after time.

As Dr. Wayne Dyer writes in his book, *The Power of Intention* (Hay House 2004), "Be the peace you're seeking from others. . . . see the light in others, and treat them as if that is all you see" (169-70). If you need love, be love. If you need compassion, be compassion. Whatever it is you want from this life, be that first. And because like attracts like, you will attract what you need once you have *become* it.

THE LAW OF PERCEPTION

Every human being is the exact center of his own life and the way he thinks and feels has a direct and all-powerful influence upon the way he interacts with others as well as his environment. We see our world not as *it is,* but as *we are.* Whatever happens or occurs is treated subjectively always. It's impossible for any of us to be objective about our own lives.

Bestselling author Richard Carlson, Ph.D. discusses precisely this in *You Can Be Happy No Matter What: Five Principles for Keeping Life in Perspective* (New World 1997).

"We have innocently learned to interpret our thoughts as if they were 'reality,' but thought is merely an ability that we have—we are the ones who produce the thoughts. It's easy to believe that because we think something, the object of our thinking (the content) represents reality (7)."

THE LAW OF THE ETERNAL PRESENT

The subconscious is geared to act, react and respond in only one time period: now. Everything it does and everything it can do, it does now, in the present. The future is only your present expectation of something that may or may not become a reality.

As Eckhart Tolle writes in his bestseller *The Power of Now: A Guide to Spiritual Enlightenment* (New World 1999):

Nothing exists outside the now. . . . What you think of as the past

*is a memory trace, stored in the mind, of a former Now. When you
remember the past, you reactivate a memory trace—and you do so
Now. The future is an imagined Now, a projection of the mind.
When the future comes, it comes as the Now. When you think
about the future, you do it now. Past and future obviously have no
reality of their own (41).*

THE LAW OF CHANGE

*Life is filled with changes. It's whether we can cope with those
changes or not that determines whether we will grow with the situation or be overcome by it . . .*

----Joan Borysenko, Ph.D., author of the
bestseller, *Minding the Body, Mending
the Mind* (Bantam 1987), p. 23.

Our creativity and efficiency are directly related to our appetite
for change. It makes sense, then, that the inability to adapt to change
causes this natural appetite to atrophy. And the result is indecision,
doubt, fear and dullness. Meanwhile, if you embrace and are willing
to adapt to change, you stimulate the creative faculty of your subconscious. And though none of us knows what is ahead, we do know that
all things pass away, and all things change. The important thing is to
use today wisely and well and face tomorrow eagerly and cheerfully.

It's also important to realize we aren't just passive victims of our
ever-changing world. We can create change if we desire to. In Louise
L. Hay's classic book, *You Can Heal Your Life* (Hay House 1987), she
discusses the process of change. She writes of the patterns that we all
have buried deep inside us, and that we must become aware of those
patterns in order to heal our overall condition. Becoming aware of
our patterns means accepting responsibility for creating the situations we are involved in and learning what we need to learn.

Once you have acknowledged the past and learned from it, it's time to release it and forgive whomever you believe has injured you. And that includes yourself. I use a technique called Release and Clear, which I'll outline later. As Louise Hay writes:

> The only thing you ever have any control over is your current thought . . . . Your old thoughts are gone; there is nothing you can do about them except live out the experiences they caused. Your current thought, the one you are thinking right now, is totally under your control (66).

In other words, you are in complete control over if, when, and to what extent you will change. The power lies within you in your thoughts. You can use your thoughts to decide to change and then to create a new behavior that you can eventually transform into a habit.

The secret of handling our changing conditions is adapting to the Natural Laws of the Mind.

Natural Laws of the Mind

The purpose of the Natural Laws of the Mind is to describe unequivocal truths about how our minds work. Once you embrace these truths, you're in a position to work *with* your mind, rather than against it. The law of electricity must be obeyed before it can become man's servant, right? When handled ignorantly, it becomes man's deadly foe. The same is true of Nature's laws. Similarly, although you might not know all of the details about how the law of electricity works, you know that it does work, and for most people, that's enough. You need only to be aware of the Natural Laws of the Mind— not how they work. Leave that part to Nature.

LAW #1

WHAT YOU THINK IS WHAT YOU GET

Any image placed into the subconscious mind develops into reality with absolute accuracy. Life is formed from the inside out; it's not determined by outward acts or circumstances. It should make sense, then, that each of us creates our own life with our thoughts. A single thought will neither make nor break a life; but a habit of thought will. You cannot think defeat and be victorious; it's impossible.

The subconscious mind responds only to mental images. It doesn't matter if the image is self-induced or from the external world. The mental image formed becomes the blueprint and the subconscious mind uses every means at its disposal to carry out the plan. Because that's true, an activity or behavior such as worrying would be the programming of an image you don't want. The subconscious, not knowing the difference between a real or imagined image, will act to fulfill the imagined situation and the things you fear most are more likely to happen.

As Wayne Dyer wrote in *Manifest Your Destiny: The Nine Spiritual Principles for Getting Everything You Want* (William Morrow 1998),

> *If your mental pictures are of being surrounded by things and conditions that you desire, and they are rooted in joy and faith, your creative thoughts will attract these surroundings and conditions into your life. . . . What you are doing is literally visualizing in detail what it is that you want to manifest . . . . You detach from the outcome and how it will be accomplished. You are not in the business of creating, but of attracting to yourself what is already in creation . . . (60).*

When you change your thoughts, you change your mind.

LAW #2
EVERY THOUGHT CAUSES
A PHYSICAL REACTION.

Our power of creation is the word. The word is the most powerful tool that humans possess. It is the tool of magic.

Don Miguel Ruiz, *The Four
Agreements Companion Book*
(Amber Allen 2000).

Your thoughts affect all of the functions of your body. For example:

- Worry thoughts trigger changes in the stomach that eventually lead to ulcers.
- Anger thoughts stimulate your adrenal glands and the increased adrenaline in the bloodstream causes many other physical changes.
- Anxiety and fear thoughts change your pulse rate.
- Hunger and thirst thoughts affect your stomach and salivary glands.
- Sex thoughts affect your sex organs.

Though personal body chemistry is guided and triggered by your emotions, it is your thought that leads the emotions. You can actually make yourself sick, poor and unhappy, just by thinking the wrong thoughts habitually. It's a law that *you become what you dwell upon*. Remember when you made yourself salivate during the Lemon Test earlier? That was your thought creating a physical reaction.

LAW #3

IMAGINATION IS MORE POWERFUL THAN KNOWLEDGE.

Images are the property of the subconscious mind (that huge 88% of your brain we discussed in Chapter One). Those images will always overpower what you think (the scant 12%). Reason is easily overruled by imagination. In fact, an idea accompanied by a strong emotion usually cannot be modified through the use of reason. However, by subconscious reprogramming, any idea can be easily and effortlessly removed, altered, or amended.

The way I teach my clients about this Natural Law of the Mind is I say: "Look at me right now. I am wearing a white shirt and navy-blue trousers, right? Okay, now close your eyes and picture me with a green shirt and purple trousers and a black hat."

"Now open your eyes and tell me which is real." Your mind doesn't know, as it has seen both and cannot tell the difference.

LAW #4

YOUR HABITS ARE YOUR LIFE

Life is full of habits. Much of your day consists of successions of actions that have become more or less automatic. Ninety-seven percent of what we do, we do by habit, spontaneously. Each separate act (habit), good or bad, plays a part in making you what you are. Fortunately, it's never too late, and you're never too old, to change your habits. You can begin today. You can begin right now, at this very moment. Remember that success is a habit and so is failure. Repetition forms positive habits and negative ones.

Men do little from reason, much from passion, most from habit.
--Dorothy Gates, Ph.D.

You Can Foretell Your Future

A surefire way to tell what your future will hold is to look at your habits of today. As I wrote earlier, if you don't change any of your habits of today, there's one place they'll inevitably lead you. For example, if you have a habit of plateauing at a certain time for the cycling leg of the triathlon, and you are aware of that plateau and remind yourself of that plateau, thereby giving a lot of energy and reinforcement to it, I guarantee you that during your next triathlon, you will plateau at the same number.

Your habits don't change by themselves; you have to do the work.

It's worth repeating: If you could change by just reading a book about change or going to therapy, everyone would be replacing all of their negative thoughts and behavior with positive ones. But it's not that easy. Reading doesn't create change easily or automatically. You need something more. Extinguishing bad habits involves cultivating new ones. And that work has to be on the subconscious level, with hypnosis.

One of the things you need to do to change a behavior is repetition. What you use increases, and what you don't use will atrophy from lack of use. All of your talents increase or decrease in proportion to the extent to which you apply them. Once a habit is formed, it becomes easier and easier to follow and more difficult to break.

In bestselling author Napoleon Hill's *Keys to Success: The 17 Principles of Personal Achievement* (Plume 1994), he refers to "The Three Essentials of Cosmic Habitforce" (209-212). What he's really talking about is how and why we form habits. The first essential is "plasticity," which is simply the ability to change which is part of our make up. The second is "frequency of impression," which means that the more you do something the faster it becomes a habit. "Repetition is the mother of habit," Hill writes.

Finally, "intensity of impression" is the third essential and means that the more concentration involved in doing something, the faster it will become a habit. "You impress the habit on your subconscious mind, and it becomes a part of everything you do."

LAW #5
DON'T BREED NEGATIVE THOUGHTS

As you probably have learned through experience, the more attention and power you give your fears, the more they affect you and the more likely they are to manifest themselves. If you continue to fear ill health, constantly talk about your "nerves," "tension headaches," "nervous stomach," in time those changes will occur, and do so quite naturally. Your nerves will act up, you'll get tension headaches, and you will experience stomach problems. All because you kept those negative notions in your mind.

This is true with any negative thought. The more you concentrate on your failures in relationships, the more likely you are to fail (in similar ways) in future relationships. In general, the more you allow fear and other negative thoughts to invade your life, the stronger their presence will become. And once they are firmly entrenched in your mind, your body will begin to create behavior to support them. You will supply physical, emotional, and mental behaviors and experiences to support the negativity you attend to.

LAW #6

ATTITUDE IS A MATTER OF CHOICE

You cannot control the external circumstances of your life, but you can control your reactions to them.

> --Joan Borysenko, Ph.D., *Minding the Body, Mending the Mind* (Bantam 1987, p. 207).

An attitude is the way you look at life, and as we've all experienced, attitudes affect the body and how it performs. Fortunately, we all have the innate ability to choose our attitude in any given set of circumstances.

The events that occur in our lives are purely neutral. That's so important to understand. Nothing is positive until we've decided it is, and it's not negative until we've decided it is. For example, I can decide to view the death of a loved one as a negative event. But death is a part of life, and perhaps that loved one's purpose had been fulfilled and now they are in a much better situation than being human on Planet Earth. When I look at it that way, I can choose to view the death as a neutral event.

In NLP, when we refer to "reframing," we are talking about the ability we all have to shift our perspective, and in turn change our approach and probably change the outcome. So the death of a loved one might, on some level be cause for grief. But it also might be cause for giving thanks. It depends on how you look at it.

LAW #7

REACTIONS MUST BE MANAGED

This law is the corollary to the previous one. Just as you can manage your attitude, you can manage your reactions. Again, what happens in your life is purely neutral. But how you react to what happens is not; it can affect your health, your relationships, and your career.

One of the more prevalent problems my clients have is the inability to handle themselves in a situation that is not comfortable for them. For instance, road rage comes up often. What do you do when you're driving along and someone cuts you off? If you are in the mindset to be angry in that nanosecond, a response of anger and aggression such as yelling, cussing, or swearing happens instantly. To be able to manage yourself is to understand why you would ever respond in such a negative, counter-productive way. Have you seen a parent or a significant other act so disproportionately angry? Have you seen the expression of road rage in a movie? Is that what you're recreating? Where did you learn your road rage? What was the anchor--the cue--that "made you" respond with road rage? Was it a car horn? A car not accelerating within a moment of a light turning green? Someone cutting you off? Once you determine what is the most common anchor for your road rage, all you have to do is repro-gram the way you react to that anchor.

> *All feelings are good, because their purpose is to provide us with*
> *information, direction, and motivation that will help us create a*
> *satisfying life.*
>   ----Calvin D. Banyan

LAW #8
THOUGHTS MUST BE KEPT ALIVE

Every thought you have must be fed and nurtured in order to keep it alive. And when your conscious mind has recognized an idea as true and guiding, it cannot simultaneously hold an opposing thought. In other words, only one idea can be entertained at one time. For example, let's say an individual believes in absolute integrity. He trains and expects his children to be honest, and he expects everyone he does business with to be honest. Meanwhile, he cheats on his income taxes. He might rationalize his conduct by saying, "Everybody else does it." He cannot, however, escape the conflict and its effect upon his nervous system that is caused by attempting to hold opposing ideas.

The following are truisms about your thoughts:

- An idea, once accepted, tends to remain until it's replaced by another idea or it's forgotten.
- Once an idea has been accepted, there's opposition to replacing it with a new idea.
- The longer an idea remains, the more opposition there is to replacing it with a new idea.
- The longer an idea remains, the more it tends to become a fixed habit of thinking. (This is how habits are formed, both good and bad ones: first the thought, then the action.)
- Therefore, if we wish to change our actions, we must begin by changing our thoughts.

LAW #9
HAVE AN ATTITUDE OF GRATITUDE

What you put forth comes back to you—and usually when it does it has gained mass and momentum. This is true of the way you treat people and even the way you deal with money. In other words, what goes around comes around. Therefore, if you develop an attitude of gratitude, and you look at your life in terms of all you have to be grateful for, you'll start seeing more to be grateful for, focusing on positive things, and more positive things will then be attracted to you.

In *Manifest Your Destiny*, Dr. Wayne Dyer writes, "The nature of gratitude helps dispel the idea that we do not have enough, that we will never have enough, and that we ourselves are not enough. . . . Gratitude is a way of experiencing the world with love rather than judgment" (149-50).

PART II

THE 6 KEYS TO AWESOME ATHLETIC PERFORMANCE

CHAPTER 4

KEY#1
CALM, COOL, & COLLECTED
YOUR PHYSICAL STATE:
FROM TENSE TO RELAXED

RELAXATION in this case means more to you than it has in the past. It's about more than letting go of your outer shell, which is controlled by your conscious mind. It's about relieving your inner core, which is controlled by your subconscious mind. It's about releasing tension deep within your body. Deep in your organs, nerves, cells, and spinal column. For many people, this will be the first time they attain such a profound state of relaxation.

The feeling of intense relaxation is enjoyable, but it's also practical; it has a purpose. When you allow yourself to relax, you also allow your subconscious to function without interference from your conscious mind. That is the state of being that is optimal for accepting suggestions that will create lasting change.

How?

By using hypnosis and the NLP anchors, you can create a change instantly. By allowing the anchor to activate, you allow yourself the response of instant relaxation. Better breathing and relaxation produce amazingly smooth communication between your brain and your body. They create the optimal environment for your muscles to do their job, without any competing messages from your brain.

Once you are relaxed, you'll experience the following:

- You'll feel more comfortable.
- Your body won't be as tense; your muscles won't be as sore.
- You'll be more aware and alert so learning can take place.
- You'll feel increasingly happy with yourself while allowing that learning to take place.
- You'll feel a sense of peace at being able to effortlessly respond and enjoy the moment.

Calm, Cool, & Collected will help you develop the art and skill of being able to relax while still feeling comfortably aware, alert and able to move fluidly.

Tension: Unrest or imbalance, often with emotional causes and physical manifestation.

Tension affects your breathing (resulting in either hyperventilation or hypoventilation to various degrees), it creates nervous shaking, it can create irregular or extreme energy (lethargy or hyperactivity), and it can even affect your memory.

And all of these negative internal experiences eventually manifest themselves physically, as thoughts and emotions cause physical reactions. When you are tense and nervous, the following tends to happen:

- The majority of tension tends to be held in the stomach, causing stiffness in the upper body, which affects rhythm.

And if your performance at your chosen sport suffers and if your upper body is stiff and lacks rhythm, tension is a serious problem.

- Tension of the body also causes tightening of the shoulders, which makes it difficult to feel the movement of a racket or club.
- Your hands tend to become stiff and clench into fists. Fixed hands lessen your ability to control whatever it is you're holding so tightly. Ironically, you aren't really feeling what you are touching when you're gripping it so tightly.
- Your gaze tends to be downward, which compromises your security and balance.

Anything you hold is an extension of your body.

Remember that a racket, club, bat, or handle bars, can only do what you do with them. Think about your mood and your stance. If you do not feel relaxed, your body will manifest your tension. What kind of tension is being sent through your arms to whatever your hands are touching?

- Nervous
- Unmanageable
- Rushing/harried
- Tentative
- Stiff

All because your mind/body connection is negatively affected by your thoughts.

Your ultimate goal is to reach the point of unconscious competence, right? You want to be so good at what you do that you aren't aware of the specific things you're doing. You want to be comfortable so you can enjoy yourself.

Take responsibility for your own stress reduction and relaxation. Here are some exercises my clients have found particularly helpful:

- Breathe.
  Find a quiet place and try to empty your mind. Breathe in deeply for 5 counts, hold your breath for 5 counts, and then exhale for 5 counts. Repeat 5 times. Paying attention to your breath helps block distractions. In fact, some people like to say to themselves, "inhale," "hold," and "exhale," or simply "in" and " out."

    Deep breathing -> increased relaxation -> slower metabolism -> muscle tension decreases -> brain waves shift from fast Beta waves, which occur during your normal waking day, to slower Alpha waves, which appear just before falling asleep.

- Focus your attention.
  Find a quiet place, sit up straight, and focus on an object. Put all of your attention on it while you inhale and exhale, slowly and deeply. When a thought comes into your mind, return to your object of attention. In just a couple of minutes, your tension will diminish, as will your anxiety. You can also do this exercise by looking at a point on the floor several feet in front of you (so your head is only slightly tilted downward), and blur your focus, so your eyes are relaxed. Again, when a thought enters your mind, return to your spot on the floor.

- Attend to your breath.

  Find a quiet place and sit in an upright position. Breathe deeply and slowly, and be aware of where your breath is most obvious. Is it in your stomach? Your chest? Your nostrils?

  Close your eyes and focus all of your attention on your breath.

  > TIP: The most effective inhale fills the stomach, then the chest, and ends with a slight lift of the shoulders. The breath moves in an upward direction. The exhale should move in the opposite direction: downward. You should exhale slowly, in a controlled manner, until you squeeze the last bit of air out of your stomach.

- Add a word.

  Next, you can add a word. In most spiritual traditions, there is a word with an "ah" or "oh" sound at the beginning, and an "mm" or "nn" sound at the end. This isn't an accident or a coincidence. These are sounds that create distinctive vibrations in your head that alter your brain waves and create a more relaxed state. Some examples are "amen," "ohm," and "shalom."

  Choose a word and repeat it to yourself, both aloud and in your head. The impact is particularly noticeable when you say your word aloud. You'll feel it vibrating in your mouth, face and head.

- Release muscle tension.

  Find a quiet place and lie down with your arms comfortably by your sides, palms up. In yoga, this is what is known as savasana, or corpse pose. Inhale and exhale, slowly, deeply, and completely, 10 times.

Bring your attention to the tips of your toes and notice if
there is any tension. If there isn't, move up your feet and
legs, in search of tension. At each location where there is
tension, bring your breath to that point. For example, if
your calves are holding tension, visualize the breath from
your inhale reaching them and filling them with healthy,
cleansing air. Then visualize them contracting, and wringing
out the air, along with any stress, tension, or pain. To make
the experience even richer, add color to this exercise. At
each place where you are holding tension, breathe until the
tension subsides, then continue scanning your body until
you have reached the top of your head, and cleared and
relaxed each point that was manifesting stress.

*TIP: Color is a powerful tool in visualization, as it has been proven
to have a dramatic effect on your emotions and your body. You can
use color when you are doing your stress management exercises,
your relaxation exercises, and your fear-management exercises.*

- *Blue is calming and relaxing. It actually physically calms the body,
  including the pulse rate, breathing, perspiration and muscle tension.*
- *Red is a powerful color that increases vitality, energy and heat. It can
  also increase the intensity of the impact of your visualizations. (Note
  that red placebos are more effective for pain relief than any other
  color!)*

*So if you want to calm yourself, visualize your breath as a blue
breeze that flows through your body. If you need energy, visualize
your breath as a red blaze shooting through your body.*

Now, let's teach you how to become *Calm, Cool, & Collected* through self-hypnosis . . .

At the beginning of *Awesome Athletic Performance* I mentioned James Braid, a surgeon from England who gave hypnosis its name and also helped gain acceptance of hypnosis in the medical community. Dr. Braid was also one of the first proponents of self-hypnosis, and believed that the power of hypnosis came not from the hypnotist, but from the mind of the person being hypnotized. Consequently, anyone who can be hypnotized by someone else, can hypnotize themselves. After all, you *allow* someone to hypnotize you—they don't *do* it *to* you.

In fact, the crucial element of directing your unconscious is *autosuggestion.* In other words, self-hypnosis is so effective because all of the suggestions for thoughts and behaviors come from the subject (i.e., you!).

As you practice, let your mind and body become more and more quiet and serene as the mental picture of soothing quiet and peaceful rest unfolds before your imagination. When relaxing, all your inner and outer muscles slacken completely. A feeling of heaviness may develop; then it may change to detachment, lightness, and indifference. A new pattern of calm, tranquil living is established.

THE SELF-HYPNOSIS SESSION

SESSION is another name for the physical act of reaching the subconscious mind. This natural technique is so effective at releasing all muscle and nerve tension within the body that you immediately experience a wonderful sense of well-being and absolute ease. This deep state of rest is accompanied by an improvement in circulation. And your mind, free from tension and useless activity, is able to strengthen and reenergize every muscle, every nerve, and every cell in the body. By releasing deep muscular tension (perhaps for the first time in your life), you alleviate nerve tension automatically. And with freedom from nerve tension comes absolute and complete relaxation.

Relaxation is achieved during the session by means of suggestion. As you relax your mind by letting it dwell upon thoughts of quietness, serenity, and well-being, your body quickly responds to the suggestion of rest by letting go and relaxing. To realize a progressively deeper state of relaxation, all you need to do is maintain this calm, quiet state of mind.

The vital point to remember in attaining the state of deep relaxation is:

Make absolutely no effort to achieve this state. No concentration or effort is necessary. Simply let it happen.

Effort is the function of the conscious mind. The subconscious mind does everything with ease. It is the subconscious you are working with during your sessions. Since it learns very quickly, your subconscious will soon anticipate what it must do so that with each repetition of the relaxation routine, you relax easier, faster and deeper.

RULES FOR SUCCESSFUL SELF-HYPNOSIS SESSIONS

When you learned to play your chosen sport, you didn't start out with perfect performance. The same is true with reaching an altered state of consciousness. You will first learn a few basic rules, and then you must practice, practice, and practice. Repetition is your friend. Repetition is the mother of mastery.

Rule #1: Preset your time limit.
Decide on a period of time you desire to relax. Twenty minutes is the research findings' best amount of time.

However, you can use five or ten minutes depending upon the circumstances.

Give your subconscious the command that under no circumstances do you exceed the time limit. Remember, it must obey you. If you find yourself exceeding that time period (especially in the beginning) it may signify that you are releasing a great amount of tension. Only in the beginning and only under extreme stress should you lengthen the time period of practice. If you must, use a clock timer to awaken you until you have trained the subconscious to respond to you. Some of you wake in the morning without a clock. This works in the same way. Your eyes will pop open, you will have a twitch or your leg will jump. Something will awaken you. You are seeking a dreamy, detached state (not sleep) wherein you can make clear and definite impressions upon your feeling mind. Total unawareness does not mean sleep. It's merely and indication that you're at a very deep level of Alpha.

Rule #2: Get comfortable.

Loosen your clothing if it's at all tight or binding. Remove your shoes, your tie, or any article of clothing that may pinch your or be uncomfortable in any way. Position yourself so that the circulation is not restricted. Arms at side, palms up, legs uncrossed, glasses or contacts removed.

Rule #3: Initially use the same place to practice.

You will begin to associate the chair, couch, bed, or even floor with the Alpha level of consciousness. As you become accustomed to the routine, habit takes over and you will find yourself propelled to that place at approximately the same

hour each day. Think of this relaxation period as you would
a daily bath—except this is a bath for your mind. If you
might be doing your self-hypnosis at work, as well, choose
a spot there and form the habit of going to that spot for
practice.

Don't use your bed if you have difficulty sleeping. Don't
use your ex-husband's or ex-wife's chair (there are negative
connotations attached). Don't practice for at least an hour
before bedtime—otherwise you will be alert and awake
when you want to sleep.

Rule #4: Use your environment.

Allow every noise, sound, or movement to carry you deeper
into the desired state. We live in a noise-filled, busy, active
world. To be completely effective you must be able to
achieve this state of Alpha any time you choose, under any
conditions. To do this, simply use your immediate environment to help you relax instead of working to discount it.
Prepare for any eventuality. If you are expecting a call, use
a telephone to awaken you. If the doorbell should ring, use
it to deepen the state. It's up to you to form the habit. Every
sound or noise can take you deeper and deeper or it can
awaken you. It's your choice.

Rule #5: Always maintain the same attitude.

Here I go! Expect to thoroughly enjoy this period of relaxation. Assume an attitude of: "I relax as deeply as I can
go and I enjoy the benefit from the experience." Avoid
analyzing, avoid questioning, and avoid attempting
anything. Simply let it happen.

AUTOMATIC RESULTS FROM PRACTICING

You sleep better, your mental and physical health improve, and your performance will improve. Without the continual carryover of tension from day to day, your system functions more efficiently. You are more at ease during both your waking and sleeping hours, and you sleep deeper and more contently, but for a shorter period of time. Twenty minutes in Alpha is equal to four hours of natural rest. When you find yourself sleeping less, you will also find yourself with extra hours to do those things you have always wanted to do—extra reading, writing, exercising, whatever interests you.

CONDITIONING YOURSELF TO REACH ALPHA STATE

Once you are able to consciously relax your mind and your body, you will be prepared to go into Alpha state using the following script. And once in Alpha, you will be ready to put yourself into a hypnotic state and accept the suggestions that will lead to changes in your behavior and performance on a deep, subconscious level.

You're probably going to have to practice a handful of times, with the complete script, in order to achieve the Alpha state that is necessary for you to accept the direct suggestions in the hypnosis script or CD. You can either read the following script or record yourself reading it (and be prepared to do it a couple of times until you get it right). Note that *Calm, Cool, & Collected* is the only one of The 6 Keys to Awesome Athletic Performance that includes this version of Alpha conditioning. Once you have successfully accessed Alpha with this extended script, you'll be ready for Instant Alpha Conditioning, where you access Alpha by using a single word of your choice.

INSTRUCTIONS FOR ALPHA CONDITIONING

1. Practice the Alpha-conditioning session for two consecutive weeks, twice a day if you can (most people do it before they go to bed at night). You may want to record it so you can do it with your eyes closed, which feels similar to what would happen if I were there with you.

2. Get comfortable. Use the same place to practice, and read (or listen to) the section on Alpha conditioning. Let it happen.

S	M	T	W	Th	F	Sat

3. After you have had at least 14 Alpha-conditioning sessions (I recommend 21), you'll be ready to learn how to access Alpha by enlisting the help of a single word. I'll explain how in a moment, but for now, let's begin retraining your brain.

ALPHA CONDITIONING

Under no circumstances do I naturally fall asleep. I allow myself to relax . . . I relax . . . and allow myself to become as comfortable as possible. I feel myself relax. I allow the sensation of gentle rest to begin flowing throughout my body. I can feel myself growing more and more relaxed . . . with each and every breath that I exhale. I visualize a balloon exhausting all its air. I too, relax, releasing greater and greater amounts of tension as I exhale . . . dissolving into the deepest state of rest. I feel . . . feel . . . the sensation of soothing relaxation as it begins in my toes . . . and each and every fiber and muscle in each toe

. . . now responds to the irresistible urge to let go . . . to let go. Each toe grows limp, loose and relaxed. As a dry sponge absorbs warm, languid liquid . . . my body absorbs the soothing, languid, glowing quietness . . . of relaxation. Irresistibly . . . the relaxation flows into both my feet. Smoothly, yet quickly, with an ever-increasing sense of pleasure . . . and enjoyment . . . the languid sense of peaceful, calm relaxation reaches my knees . . . and my knees relax. Swiftly now, like that thirsty sponge . . . soaking up warm, languid liquid . . . the relaxation spreads to my upper legs . . . saturating them . . . spreading smoothly into both hips, and I am, from the hips all the way down . . . to the tips of my toes . . . firmly aware . . . and yet deeply relaxed.

With every breath now, my level of conscious awareness grows less . . . and less . . . and less. Feeling safe and secure, my legs seem to fade . . . fade . . . fade away. Every breath is slow and easy . . . slow and easy . . . slow and easy. As I relax deeper and deeper, the same soothing . . . tingling. . . relaxation . . . now begins to develop in my fingertips . . . filling each finger smoothly, deeply, and totally, with the sensation of deep relaxation. Each finger discharges every last bit of muscular tension . . . and in doing so . . . grows limp, loose and relaxed. As the relaxation grows deep and complete . . . it spills over into both of my hands . . . saturating every tissue . . . every fiber . . . every cell . . . with the most enjoyable sensation . . . of absolute ease and quietness. As tension is dissipated, I become aware . . . of the sensation of the free-flowing circulation of the blood . . . which adds to the glow of relaxation. Both my hands are now completely relaxed . . . and the relaxation spreads with increasing effectiveness . . . into my wrists . . . and my wrists let go . . . into my forearms . . . and they, too, grow limp and relaxed. My elbows let go as they, too . . . seem to fade . . . fade . . . fade away.

Swiftly now, the glowing sensation of utter calmness and tranquility permeates my upper arms . . . the muscles grow limp and relaxed . . . and finally permeates both shoulders and . . . my shoulders let go . . . very limp, very relaxed. With each soothing, satisfying breath, they seem to fade . . . fade . . . fade . . . from my conscious awareness. My legs are deeply relaxed . . . my arms are deeply relaxed. A soothing . . . penetrating . . . deep quietness of my arms and legs now begins to penetrate, to saturate . . . to fill and to soak . . . the rest of my body . . . with calm, quiet rest. I visualize clear, golden honey flowing smoothly and gently . . . into a clear, glass container. Like the honey, the relaxation spills down from my shoulders, flows down my spinal column . . . bubbling up from my hips . . . and through my body . . . slowly filling with the most pleasant . . . enjoyable sensation of quietness. My back muscles relax . . . my abdomen muscles relax . . . my chest muscles relax . . . and every tissue . . . every organ . . . every gland, deep within my being responds to this soothing sensation . . . by relaxing also. Relax . . . relax . . . relax.

Every sound, every noise, every voice that I hear helps me to relax deeper and deeper. My glands and my organs are smoothly and efficiently . . . growing even more relaxed . . . with each and every beat of my heart. My heart is now pumping soothing . . . easy . . . quietness throughout my being. Slowly and irresistibly now . . . my entire body is filling . . . filling . . . filling . . . with relaxation . . . and soon, my entire body grows limp . . . and then begins to fade . . . fade . . . fade away. As my conscious mind yields to its critical authority . . . as it drifts . . . and dreams . . . and floats . . . the irresistible sensation of relaxation spreads smoothly into the muscles of my neck . . . and each nerve . . . each muscle . . . each fiber . . . grows limp and relaxes . . . responding more and more to the urge to relax . . . deeper and deeper. As my neck muscles relax . . . all congestion is relieved . . . all tension vanishes . . . and the sensation of utter contentment fills my mind. My mind urges my relaxed body to let go even more. The soothing quietness spreads into my scalp . . . and my entire scalp lets go.

A blanket of quietness is slowly enveloping my entire being, which I can now feel. I feel a cap of soothing, drowsy rest spreading over my entire scalp . . . and with such ease . . . with such enormous pleasure . . . the languid warmth finally spreads down across my face . . . and every muscle . . . every nerve . . . every fiber in my face grows limp and relaxed. The muscles in my cheeks and jaws let go. I am now completely and totally relaxed. Every breath takes me deeper and deeper. Every breath finds me with less . . . and less conscious awareness, but with greater and greater receptivity of my subconscious mind. I am, from this time forward, growing more relaxed . . . serene . . . and calm during all my waking and sleeping hours. I can, at any time, achieve this same deep sense of relaxation and quietness. I have the ability to relax and I do so . . . with the greatest ease and pleasure . . . making relaxation the easiest thing I do.

Upon awakening . . . I find I am more refreshed . . . and more invigorated . . . than I have ever felt before in my whole life. I always find relaxation refreshing . . . invigorating . . . rejuvenating.

TWENTY MINUTES. WIDE AWAKE.

Once you have completed the above program, you can progress to a more immediate form of Alpha conditioning . . .

INSTRUCTIONS FOR INSTANT ALPHA CONDITIONING

Assuming you did the extended Alpha script, for 14-21 times, under the proper conditions, you should easily be able to progress from the extended script to accessing Alpha state by using a single word (you meditators out there will already be familiar with this process, and whatever mantra you currently use will work just fine for our purposes here).

1. Select a word you would like to use to replace the Alpha conditioning technique introduced above.
2. Practice this for one week. If Alpha state occurs when you use the chosen word, go on with the program. If not, repeat this set of instructions until Alpha occurs, using your chosen word. When Alpha consistently occurs, you can use this technique to prepare your mind prior to any of the self-hypnosis scripts.

Instant Alpha Conditioning

From this moment on, each and every time I desire to attain the deep state of total relaxation, I am instantly and fully relaxed, as I am now drifting into the Alpha state of consciousness. The moment I think my chosen word _____, Alpha occurs. This word has an effect only when I use it and only under the proper circumstances. Each and every time I do use it I am fully prepared to receive positive, beneficial and constructive suggestions, impressing each one deeper into the storage and memory facility of my brain.

From this moment on, _____ triggers deep relaxation of my mind and body. I feel Alpha occur. I feel wonderful. I feel comfortable. I am totally receptive and responsive to my own creative ideas and suggestions. I am bathed in a glow of quietness, peace, and serenity. My chosen word works only when I deliberately use it for deep relaxation to attain Alpha consciousness. Its use in regular conversation has no effect on me whatsoever. From this moment on, each and every time I desire the deep state of total relaxation, I am instantly and fully relaxed upon saying _____. Because my subconscious must follow my command, each and every time I desire total relaxation, I am instantly and fully relaxed when I think my chosen word_____. I feel a deep sense of gratification as this word programming becomes a reality. Feeling wonderful, generous, alive, and eager to become Calm, Cool, & Collected.

Please note that the last few words of Instant Alpha for each Key will be unique to that Key. Once you are able to easily access Alpha using your word, your technique will be to:

1. Access Alpha using Instant Alpha.
2. Proceed immediately to the script for *Calm, Cool & Collected, Positive Self-Talk, Gaining Concentration,* or whichever of The 6 Keys to Awesome Athletic Performance you are working on.

The Power of Compounding

At the end of each script you'll notice a sentence that looks something like this:

This entire suggestion is represented by the letter "R" of my sub-key word "RHYTHM." Anytime I think, say, or see the word "RHYTHM," all suggestions keyed to this word are automatically activated, stimulated and work for my benefit.

Each of the 6 Keys is associated to a letter in RHYTHM. This technique is called compounding, the effect of which is that each time you see, hear, or say the word RHYTHM, all of the effects of your sessions are triggered and made exponentially more powerful. You need to remember the word RHYTHM at least once every 36 hours to get the full effect.

R   21 sessions of *Calm, Cool, & Collected*

H   21 Sessions of *Positive Self-Talk*

Y   21 Sessions of *Gaining Concentration*

T   21 Sessions of *Release of Performance Anxiety*

H   21 Sessions *Mastering Fear*

M   21 Sessions *Achieving Peak Performance*

After this has all been put into the subconscious mind you will be able to feel the results. Let's begin at the beginning for Calm, Cool, & Collected. . .

First, do Instant Alpha, which ends with "eager to become Calm, Cool, & Collected," and then go immediately to this script (or CD) . . .

Calm, Cool, & Collected

When I am practicing or competing, I feel so relaxed . . . I enjoy my sport and it makes me feel so good. I feel relaxed when I'm getting prepared . . . I automatically feel so comfortable and relaxed when I put on my athletic gear. I am able to perform well . . . I am able to be peaceful and alert while I am practicing or competing. Because I am calm and relaxed, I perform better. I do whatever task I need to do with such confidence, relaxation and ease. Everything I do comes so easy to me. I find that because I am calm and relaxed my body responds better. My body moves with complete balance . . . I handle everything that I do with great confidence and self-assurance.

I am very calm and peaceful. I feel great. I completely enjoy the wonderful feeling of being completely relaxed. Relaxation comes to me so easily, so much so that should I try to resist relaxation consciously or subconsciously, my body automatically grows more relaxed. I continue to relax even more soundly and more deeply with every breath that I exhale. I enjoy all these sensations that allow me to relax without any effort whatsoever. My whole body just gives in. The more and more I allow my body to relax, the better I feel. The better I feel, the more and more my body relaxes.

In every way now I feel better, happier and more content. Every second, every minute, every hour, every day, my self-confidence builds more and more. I have a positive attitude. My mind stays calm and content in all situations. I have the ability to let everything flow in peace and harmony with my new way of enjoying life. I have good thinking and good judgment ... always relaxed and able to handle all events in my life with the ability to let everything happen in a peaceful content way.

When I am on the court or field or trail or pool, I feel relaxed. My athletic performance feels so good because I am at peace with myself. I am calm and I perform well . . . I do whatever task I need to do with such confidence and ease. Everything I do comes so easy to me. I am calm and relaxed. I feel so comfortable that I move my body with complete balance and ease. I handle everything that I do with such confidence.

I feel so marvelous and wonderful every time I practice or compete . . . these wonderful feelings stay with me all the time . . . every day. I am happy and content and I give in to the potential of my mind and body. Whatever my mind can conceive, my body can achieve. How great I feel . . . how peaceful. All of these suggestions help and guide me to be more and more relaxed every time I practice or compete. I allow my body to relax and to enjoy these wonderful, good feelings that go through my body.

Anytime I desire to feel better than I do, I simply take a moment

. . . take a couple of deep breaths, and say the word "relax" quietly to myself. The word "relax" is a conditioned response key to my subconscious mind. When I say this word, I recapture the feelings of being comfortable and relaxed while I was preparing to compete. I feel enthusiastic about my future. The word "relax" is my conditioned suggestion. Every time I use my relaxation programming, it becomes more effective. Each time I say the word "relax," I move with harmony, comfort and relaxation.

Every time I have a lesson or I practice, I feel more and more confident. I am in balance and enjoy myself. I am automatically relaxed when I'm practicing or competing. This makes me feel so confident, relaxed and secure.

This entire suggestion is represented by the letter "R" of my sub-key word "RHYTHM." Anytime I think, say, or see the word "RHYTHM," all suggestions keyed to this word are automatically activated, stimulated and work for my benefit.

You now have the choice to either awaken or to drift off into a normal, natural sleep. If you are going to awaken, say:

Twenty minutes. Wide awake.

If you are going to drift off into a normal, natural sleep, say:

I am now going to drift off into a normal, natural sleep. When I awaken, I will feel fully rested, calm, and at peace with myself, the world, and those around me.

CHAPTER 5

KEY #2
POSITIVE SELF-TALK
YOUR INNER MONOLOGUE: FROM NEGATIVE TO EMPOWERING

AS your own most important critic, it is crucial to your success that you teach yourself to recognize unfair self-criticism and turn it into empowering self-talk. Practicing empowering self-talk and working on your mindset is actually just as important as practicing the technical aspects of your sport. The same way that the technical aspects take practice, so do mental ones.

Some of my clients find it extremely helpful to write little reminders, goals and affirmations on note cards and place these cards where they can see them at the start of their day. If you're having trouble with your mindset, try making one that says, "I am relaxed and confident every time I grip my racket/put on my uniform/ whatever." Repeat this phrase to yourself often and with a lot of enthusiasm. Before you know it, you'll notice an improvement in your performance!

The Little Competitor That Could

My clients often express frustration that they possess identical, if not superior, physical attributes to their competition, yet they're consistently being outperformed by that competition. In many of these cases, the factor that separates their performance from the competition is that they're operating with a limiting belief about their athletic ability and the level of performance they are capable of achieving. Their resulting, flawed performance is evidence that an individual's core beliefs will ultimately determine the reality they manifest.

"I think I can, I think I can, I think I can . . ." said the Little Engine That Could as he chugged up the mountain. More than just a children's story, this is a valuable lesson. *What we tell ourselves has a profound impact on our performance.* In fact, in my experience, the single most important and effective thing that any player can do to improve their performance is to change negative self-talk into positive, empowering self-talk.

Whatever the mind can conceive, and believe, it can achieve.
Napoleon Hill, Think and Grow Rich

Self-Talk Defined

Self-talk is exactly what it sounds like. It's your internal monologue – the words you use when you talk to yourself either in your own mind or out loud.

It's been established by neuroscientists and psychologists that most people carry on an ongoing monologue, or self-talk, of between 150 and 300 words per minute. Most of this self-talk consists of the mundane, routine and harmless thoughts we all have such as "I'm hungry," or "I need to get my hair cut soon."

The danger for players and other athletes is when this internal dialogue takes on a negative connotation such as, "I'll never be as good as s/he is." When this kind of self-talk becomes ongoing, you create limiting beliefs about yourself and about your abilities that may, if left unchecked, go on to become self-fulfilling prophecies.

For those of you who are academic-minded, consider Expectancy Theory (and the Placebo Effect): You don't always get what you want, or what you work for, but you will more often than not get what you expect. If you expect to miss a hit, you will. If you don't expect to properly execute a swing, you won't.

If you think that negative self-talk isn't really that big of a problem in the athletic world, check in on any number of sports-related discussion forums on the Internet. You won't need to read long before coming across a fellow player asking for help with some technique or another while at the same time berating him or herself constantly and saying things like, "I just can't do it!" or "I never get that right!"

There are many self-talk mistakes that athletes commonly make when preparing for and playing in a match/tournament/race/game/competition. Fortunately, all of them are easily dealt with, as you'll see in a moment. Among them are:

- *Focusing on the past or future.*
  "I never play well when I play in this tennis tournament. Most of the times I have played in this tournament I've hit the ball into the net!" This is a classic example of not letting go of past mistakes. It's just as counterproductive to worry about what *might* happen. As a player, you can always have complete control over the present moment, and that's where your thoughts need to be.

- *Thinking only of the outcome.*
  "I have to win," or any other thought about outcome isn't
  a good use of your mental energy, as outcome is something
  that you have little control over. What you do have control
  over, however, is performance. Try changing your self-talk
  to focus on what needs to be done to produce your best
  possible performance, and trust that the outcome will take
  care of itself.

- *Focusing on outside factors beyond your control.*
  "I hate running when it's windy," or, "I never do well when
  there are people in my group talking business for the whole
  game." These types of thoughts are a waste of your mental
  energy and can only hurt your confidence and therefore your
  performance. Work your hardest to keep your thoughts on
  controllable factors.

- *Focusing on weaknesses.*
  The time to focus on your weaknesses is during practice or
  when you're working with your coach. It's necessary during
  these times to identify where your weaknesses are and then
  work to improve them. On the other hand, dwelling on
  weaknesses *during* competition only serves to hurt your
  confidence and make you more nervous and tentative.

- *Demanding perfection.*
  Avoid saying to yourself: "This needs to be a perfect race,"
  or berating yourself for small mistakes. All athletes make
  mistakes, but it's the really great ones who can make a
  mistake and continue their performance unfazed. It's great
  to work towards a perfect play/serve/return/race if that's

what motivates you, but it's unrealistic to expect to deliver perfection every time out.

Though I have difficulty with the word "perfect," I have seen perfect plays or swings and I may even have had some. And if you've had some moments of perfection, make sure you use those memories when you are visualizing, as you will be increasing the probability that they will recur. "Perfection," however, is a different ballgame. Perfection assumes that no matter what you do, there is some other, higher level that you are working toward but that, by definition, you'll never achieve. The idea of perfection makes people drive and strive and exhaust themselves, only to constantly feel inadequate and self-critical.

If you want to demand something of yourself, demand that you do the best you can at each moment.

How to Change Your Self-Talk

Chances are you've experienced a few of the above self-talk mistakes in the past. But how do you actually change your self-talk to be more positive? We can't really control the thoughts that come into our heads, right?

Wrong.

There are two ways to eliminate negative self-talk. One is through a process commonly referred to as *thought-stopping*, which involves four steps:

1. Become aware of self-talk.
2. Stop the negative.
3. Replace with positive.

4. Practice the act of stopping negative thoughts.

Easy enough, right?

The only problem is that for thought-stopping to be effective, it requires lots and lots of practice on the conscious level. The way we think and talk to ourselves can be a terribly hard habit to break, considering we've been doing it a certain way for our entire lives. To improve your inner monologue this way, you need to work hard to learn to recognize when you're engaging in negative self-talk, then you need to work equally hard at stopping those thoughts and replacing them with positive ones. Fortunately, there's an easier, faster way of changing your self-talk.

Lemme guess . . . does it involve hypnosis?

Yes. The second way that you can eliminate your negative self-talk requires very little effort at all because you use your subconscious mind. Your subconscious mind is what tells you that you need to stop at a red light, or to pedal the bike to make it go, or even to breathe. These are actions that, over time, cease to require conscious thought and seem to happen on their own. In truth it's your subconscious (remember, which makes up about 88% of your mind!) that takes care of these things for you.

Creating Positive Self-Talk

Despite the fact that there are close to one million words in English, we use only a fraction of them (just a couple thousand, on average). I suggest doing some vocabulary building, and while you're at it, some weeding out, as well. There are a handful of words that most people frequently use, which affect the subconscious so negatively that my opinion is that we could all benefit from eliminating them from our vocabularies. Before we discuss what your self-talk should look like, let's first address the most important words to avoid when you're talking to yourself or to anyone else.

WORDS TO AVOID

- **Try**

  Try is one of the most poisonous words in the English language. This venomous little word can cause much misery. TRY means to test, to attempt to do something. But its connotation is deadly, as it creates three reactions in the subconscious.

  1. It programs failure. If at first you don't succeed, try, try . . . again. The ellipse between "try" and "again" means over and over again. Failure is implicit in the word try. I tried to lose weight (but failed). I tried to be a good father (but failed). I tried to remember what the coach told me to do during practice (but failed).

  2. Try is a wholly negative word. Because life requires a total commitment, and because try gives you an ideal out to escape responsibility for doing or not doing something, it is the word many people hide behind. They refuse to commit themselves to yes or no. It's so easy to seek the middle ground and say "I'll try" whether you want to or not. As you utter the word try, your subconscious immediately picks it up and says FAIL. Listen to people who use the word TRY a lot. Invariably, they are failure-oriented and frustrated.

  3. TRY is not an action word. It doesn't give you anything

to do. For instance, you hear the word sing, run, or sit, and your processor gives you something to do with them. Now do that with the word try. What are you going to do with try?

Replace self-defeating talk with "I'll do my best."

- **Hope**

  Every word you speak or hear causes a certain kind of emotional and physical response. HOPE transmits a subconscious image, which promotes a feeling of anxiety—the subtle dread that something bad is about to happen. "I hope I get this point" creates a negative response. There is an unhealthy feeling and there is serious doubt about what you know or, at the very least, an uncertainty about the outcome of that test. This emotional response takes place without your conscious awareness because our emotions are rooted in the subconscious.

- **Problem**

  When you use the word PROBLEM you are emphasizing an obstacle and generating a feeling of helplessness; that's why this word is so lethal and every self-help guru will tell you to eliminate it from your vocabulary. If you dwell on difficulties, barriers, or defects, the nonselective, subjective mind accepts your thinking as your command and then proceeds to work strenuously to produce the same in your external world. Replace problem with something like "challenge."

- **Can't**

> Bobby, age 8: *Mrs. Siegal, can I go to the bathroom?*
> Mrs. Siegal: *I don't know Bobby, can you?*

I remember that same exchange occurring over and over again when I was in grammar school. It was actually a great technique for reminding us kids that "can" means that you physically have the ability to do something. And "can't," therefore, means that you are physically unable to do something. That is a very powerful, very negative concept, and might not be an accurate one.

When you say "can't" you often mean "won't," which implies you have made a conscious decision to opt out. My suggestion is to say what you mean. If you mean "I choose not to," say so. After all, most people know that when you say "I can't" you really mean "I won't," anyway, and they'll appreciate your honesty.

- **Not**

Have you ever told yourself, "I will not hit the ball into the water . . . I will not hit the ball into the water . . . I will not hit the ball into the water," and then hit the ball into the water? We've all repeated similar phrases and had the same outcome: disappointment. Why? Because the subconscious is incapable of producing the word "not" in your behavior. Instead, it produces everything but "not." So it produces the behavior that supports "I will hit the ball into the water." Need more proof? Quick—do not think of a yellow polar bear sitting next to you. What happened?

Your knowledge of how your subconscious deals with (or

doesn't deal with) negative words like "not," "don't," and "won't," will be especially useful when you're constructing affirmations for yourself. But as for your daily language, starting today, always state the outcome you desire in the positive, such as, "I am going to hit this ball right onto the green (or better yet, into the hole!)."

THE TWO MOST POWERFUL WORDS YOU CAN USE

- **I am**

  These three letters, when put together like this—I am—are a powerful tool for both negative and positive self-talk. *Why?* Because your subconscious will assume the identity of whatever follows them. Consider "I am so fat" and "I am in great shape." If you were to rearrange those sentences, you'd end up with "So fat, I am." "In great shape, I am." It implies that you and the state of being you describe are inextricable. You and "so fat" are the same thing; you are one. So if you are trying to lose weight, you will have a very difficult time, as you are carrying around with you the very obstacle you seek to eliminate.

TIPS FOR IMPROVING YOUR AUTOSUGGESTIONS (I.E., YOUR LANGUAGE)

Here are some simple rules to follow when structuring your language—to yourself or to others. You can also use these rules when you are creating affirmations or suggestions when writing your own self-hypnosis script for your specific athletic endeavor (or anything you'd like to accomplish). Remember that your language creates action in the world and that language (both negative and positive) programs your subconscious. And when you're in Alpha state, your language will program your subconscious very quickly, and very easily, so as they say, *"Be careful what you wish for . . . "*

1. Be realistic. Though your subconscious mind doesn't recognize the concept of impossible, and will work on anything, there are five areas to avoid, particularly when you are in Alpha state.

    a. Avoid working on the mind of another. The one mind you know you can control is your own. Besides, the universe doesn't reward people who try to control the minds of others.

    b. Avoid attempting to change the orderly progression of time.

    c. Avoid thinking you can call upon knowledge, information, and experience you don't have (e.g., you can't fly, you don't have bionic vision or hearing, and, no offense, your swing isn't identical to that of Serena Williams).

    d. Avoid the attempt to make physical changes that are physically impossible (e.g., although some nonhuman animals can regrow limbs, we cannot. And although I have heard people tell me they used affirmations to increase their bust size, I'm a bit wary of this technique.)

    e. Avoid manipulation of that which is beyond your control (e.g., the weather).

2. Phrase everything in the present time. "I will" means later and later never comes. Create a strong mental picture of

your objective "NOW" and let your subconscious produce it for you.

3. Always use a completely non-resistant (positive) approach. Make no mention of what is bothering you. Create a dynamic and positive image of your objective. Talking about what you don't want and visualizing what you don't want just makes what you don't want more likely to occur.

4. State your objective clearly. Know exactly what you want. Fuzzy, hazy goals produce little in the way of results. Always work for the strongest possible response—feelings and pictures.

5. Stress activity. You must begin where you are NOW. Stress the activity toward your objective. Visualize your active participation.

6. Visualize. Remember that Alpha consciousness responds only to mental images. So when you're in Alpha, picture the desired goal as you produce Alpha brainwaves. Let the image happen. Thinking is conscious-mind activity, and when you think, you should be restricting yourself to positive, productive thoughts and images.

7. Symbolize. Any concept, goal, or objective that doesn't lend itself easily to visualization can be readily impressed into the subconscious mind by simply assigning a symbol to it. For example, whenever anyone says "ball," an image appears in your consciousness. You probably see a specific ball, and with it you then have a feeling of delight, a feeling of anger, a "blah" feeling, a feeling of excitement—any number of responses can be triggered according to your experiences. In this same manner, you can deliberately use words, colors, objects, people and things to trigger entire affirmations and/ or suggestions.

Here are some examples of helpful affirmations that my clients often use:

- I handle stress and tension appropriately and effectively.
- My mood is calm and relaxed.
- I cope well and get on with my life during times of stress.
- My breathing is deep, slow and calm.
- I am a confident player.

SAM'S STORY

Sam's story is a great illustration of how you can reprogram yourself to let go of negative memories, clear your mind, and develop a positive, productive internal language that will lead to a better mental state and better performance.

When Laura asked me why I was going to see her I had no problem responding. I've got a big problem and now know what it is. I am very critical of my results. I find I will begin to tell myself negative things on the tennis court once I start to get results I am not looking for. I seem to have ingrained in my head things like, "There's no way you'll make that shot with that swing," or "You're not good enough to make that volley—you'll hit it into the net like you always do. "

I feel especially bad because now I have this great coach who's really positive and supportive. But as soon as he stops talking to me for a minute, or is silent when I execute a good volley on my own, my mind instantly gets negative and critical. I usually then regress back to what's comfortable (but not right) and my old swing takes over, which is exactly what I am trying to change.

I can't expect my coach, or anyone else for that matter, to have to talk me through my game all the time like I am a child. I know better than that, but I sometimes do feel like a child who has been told his whole life that he can't do anything right, and negative thoughts replay in my mind. I understand I have experience with bad results that might reinforce why I feel like I am heading the wrong way again. But this is part of why I am changing my swing. Why is it so hard for this to happen for me?

Clearly, Sam had some challenges based on his prior experiences. *My* challenge was to retrain his brain by removing the old, destructive patterns and thoughts that were conditioned responses, and replacing them with words and imagery that would create optimistic internal language and lead to peak performance. Basically, Sam had developed a habit of thinking a certain way, and we needed to replace the thinking in that habit with content that was positive and empowering.

The following tips are helpful to anyone, in any situation, who is paralyzed by the memories or the effects of the past.

- Disengage the negative thoughts and patterns from your subconscious mind so you can move forward. (I use a technique called Release and Clear, which will be detailed in a moment.)
- Change your perspective of the past by gathering new information. (I use reframing for this.)
- Create an image of the desired performance. This image acts as a road map of the correct, optimal swing for the shot you're about to hit, for instance. (I use Theater of the Mind to accomplish this.)

- Instantly trigger a desired response by using an anchor. For example, I told Sam that every time he steps up to the ball he is relaxed and every time he holds the racket, he is alert, breathes rhythmically and performs at his peak level.
- Provide a real-life example of someone who has reached the desired level of competence. (I use Modeling to create this.)
- Surround yourself with people, sights, and sounds that contribute to high-level performance. (I use the Circle of Excellence.)
- Develop a new language to be used for internal thinking and external speech, which will eventually create behavior that is consistent with the language.

Let's look at how one simple word can powerfully transform your self-talk. After hypnotizing Sam and introducing him to the CANCEL technique . . .

I realize now what I was doing wrong. I was setting myself up to make mistakes because I was thinking a negative thought. Laura hypnotized me to say the word CANCEL and immediately replace the negative thought with a positive one. Now, when a negative thought enters my mind, it's so easy to just cancel out that thought. Eliminating negative thinking from my thought processes has changed my whole tennis experience. Now I fill my mind with positive thoughts, and I get positive results. It was so easy to change the way I was thinking. Laura told me that every time I see the color red I think positive thoughts about my playing ability. As a reminder to be positive, I bought a red tennis bag, so every time I pull out my racket I see the color red and it triggers the positive thought needed to repeat the good tempo required for a good swing.

I've always been one of those people who really believed in Murphy's

Law, always thinking about the negative and always prepared for it. But now I find that I need to concentrate on the outcome and keep it positive and visualize it. I am what I think. And I am choosing to be positive. And that has completely changed my game.

SELF-HYPNOSIS TO TRANSFORM YOUR SELF-TALK

INSTANT ALPHA CONDITIONING

Instructions:

1) Use the word you selected to replace the Alpha conditioning technique introduced in *Calm, Cool, & Collected*. Read the following script and let Alpha occur.
2) Then proceed to the script for Release and Clear and/or Positive Self-Talk.

From this moment on, each and every time I desire to attain the deep state of total relaxation, I am instantly and fully relaxed, as I am now drifting into the Alpha state of consciousness. The moment I think my chosen word _____, Alpha occurs. This word has an effect only when I use it and only under the proper circumstances. Each and every time I do use it I am fully prepared to receive positive, beneficial, and constructive suggestions, impressing each one deeper into the storage and memory facility of my brain.

From this moment on, _____ triggers deep relaxation of my mind and body. I feel Alpha occur. I feel wonderful. I feel comfortable. I am totally receptive and responsive to my own creative ideas and suggestions. I am bathed in a glow of quietness, peace, and serenity. My chosen word works only when I deliberately use it for deep relaxation to attain Alpha consciousness. Its use in regular conversation has no effect on me whatsoever. From this moment on, each and every time I desire the deep state of total relaxation, I am instantly and fully relaxed upon saying _____. Because my subconscious must follow my command, each and every time I desire total relaxation, I am instantly and fully relaxed when I think my chosen word_____. I feel a deep sense of gratification as this word programming becomes a reality. Feeling wonderful, generous, alive, and eager to Release and Clear negative thoughts and move on to creating Positive Self-Talk.

RELEASE AND CLEAR

If negative thoughts, memories, or other images tend to creep into your mind and invade your thinking while you are playing, this simple technique will help release your mind from thinking about (or even obsessing over) those negatives so you can move on and use your brain for more productive things.

Instructions:

1) Read each night, before retiring, for 21 nights. If you miss a night, you must begin again. Read aloud, with feeling.

S	M	T	W	Th	F	Sat

2) Say the words Release and Clear every night thereafter.

RELEASE AND CLEAR

So relaxed . . . so relaxed . . . slowly drifting into a most satis-fying state of relaxation. Relaxation is good for me. I release every last ounce of useless tension . . . as I rest contentedly, to awaken when I must, refreshed and invigorated. I am alive with the feeling of freedom, of promise, of exhilarating positive expectation. My mind is clear . . . my body recharged . . . and my past deactivated . . . and left behind me.

As I relax . . . I release every unhappy experience of the past . . . and everything connected with those experiences. I find it easy to let them go. I am a part of life . . . as are we all . . . and we all move, live, and think, as we have a right to. Life goes on, and so do I . . . growing rich in experience . . . and in capacity to achieve. My positive experi-ences supply me with a directness to meet the challenges of my life. All I must do is use the amazing power of my subconscious mind. I am using that capacity now to disengage me from every negative . . . destructive . . . and harmful impression ever made upon me. They fade . . . fade . . . fade out of my life forever.

I am grateful and thankful for every experience of the past. I now forgive myself for every mistake I have every made; and I forgive everyone else who may have in any way harmed me. I know that out of each experience . . . as I understand it . . . good must surely come to me. I forgive myself for every mistake because I know that each mistake is a steppingstone to greater understanding . . . to greater opportunity . . . and to greater achievement. I grow stronger with each experience . . . and I am stronger than anything life can offer. I am preparing myself to meet its challenges directly . . . free of nega-tive conditioning. I am more than any challenge . . . for I possess the power and the ability to channel any experience into a rich and rewarding way of life.

I now fully release the past . . . and all its effects upon me. I am free . . . free of the past . . . free to be me . . . entirely. I accept myself completely. I am a valuable and talented human being . . . I am always aware of my innate worth. There are things to be done by me . . . that are done better by me than by any other human being. Every word . . . every movement . . . every gesture of mine . . . preserves my unique stamp upon life. For as long as time has been . . . or ever shall be . . . there is no one who can exactly duplicate me. I am pleased . . . I accept myself . . . I love myself . . . I am grateful for my new level of understanding. My acceptance releases me from self-dislike . . . and so I am now free to change that which must be changed . . . to improve that which can be improved . . . to let go of that which is inhibiting or destructive. My self-acceptance now enables me to accept everyone else . . . I accept myself . . . I accept others as they are . . . I accept even those who are unacceptable . . . as unacceptable . . . and go on my way.

I bestow upon others my affection . . . true and unencumbered. In my imagination . . . I see them having all the good I desire for myself. What I desire for myself, I also desire for everyone else . . . I have fulfilled my nature. I have supplied myself with those priceless qualities and feelings . . . acceptance . . . love . . . and forgiveness . . . and so I now have them to give. I give them freely. I feel the warmth and excitement of building a new and rewarding life. A firm, quiet sense of self-love and self-determination dominates my every waking and sleeping hour. I am ready to release, and do so this night. CLEAR . . . CLEAR . . . CLEAR.

Once you've done the instant Alpha and then Release and Clear if you needed it, proceed to self-hypnosis for positive self-talk.

POSITIVE SELF-TALK

When negative thoughts enter my mind about my athletic performance, I mentally say the word "CANCEL." I replace any negative thought that I may have with a positive thought. Positive thoughts remain within the conscious portion of my mind much longer and much clearer than ever before. Without fail, without exception, without excuse, each and every time a negative thought or idea enters my mind, I mentally say the word "CANCEL" to myself. My personal life is in order, my private life is content, and my health is in perfect order. I see myself how I want to be. I am positive, happy, healthy and glad to be alive.

I know that being positive, happy, healthy and glad to be alive is called being "in the zone." I am in the zone when I am on the (insert your venue "field," "court," "slopes," etc.). I understand that being "in the zone" is when I feel that I am winning all of the time . . . it is an unstoppable, powerful confidence that means that I am the best that I can be. I am always absolutely doing and achieving what I set my mind to do. I am thankful that through the power of positive thinking I have the ability to create positive actions. My internal positive self-talk allows me to achieve whatever outcomes I want to work towards. I know that when I practice positive self-talk, my subconscious mind allows positive, empowering thoughts to flow through to my conscious mind.

Every day that I'm engaged in my sport, I am physically stronger and fitter. I am more alert, more wide-awake, and more energetic. Every day that I leave the house to practice, I remain deeply interested in whatever I am doing. When I am playing, running or swimming, my mind is much less preoccupied with myself and I am much less conscious of myself. I focus on the task at hand. Every day that I work out, my nerves are stronger and steadier. When I begin my practice my mind is calm, clear and composed. I think clearly . . . I concentrate easily . . . my memory is sharp . . . I see things in their true perspective and do not allow them to get out of proportion. Every day I spend time practicing or competing, I am emotionally calm and tranquil. I feel a wonderful sense of personal well-being, personal safety, and security. I am completely relaxed and tranquil. I have confidence in myself and in my athletic ability. I am optimistic, happy, and confident. I stick up for myself . . . I stand on my own feet . . . I hold my own ground. Things happen exactly as I wish for them to happen during my athletic performances, during practice, at home, and at work. I remain cheerful and optimistic.

No matter what is going on in my life, I always remain positive and free from negative self-talk. I am confident in my athletic abilities and "CANCEL" out any negative and harmful self-talk that I may have. I remain with a clear outlook for a wonderful and successful future in and out of athletic competition. Every time I see the color red, it reminds me that I will be positive and in the zone.

This entire suggestion is represented by the letter "H" of my sub-key word "RHYTHM." Anytime I think, say, or see the word "RHYTHM," all suggestions keyed to this word are automatically activated, stimulated and work for my benefit.

You now have the choice to either awaken or to drift off into a normal, natural sleep. If you are going to awaken, say:

Twenty minutes. Wide awake.

If you are going to drift off into a normal, natural sleep, say:

I am now going to drift off into a normal, natural sleep. When

I awaken, I will feel fully rested, calm, and at peace with myself, the world and those around me.

CHAPTER 6

KEY #3
GAINING CONCENTRATION
YOUR FOCUS: FROM
SCATTERED TO OPTIMAL

Concentration upon a single idea has been the hallmark of success for countless people and organizations. The single idea you want to concentrate your attention on is something like: achieve peak performance in my game or competition.

PEOPLE with concentration challenges usually talk a lot about having difficulty "staying focused." They are easily distracted by:

- The other competitors around them.
- Other matches on the court or field next to them.
- The person talking on their phone near them.
- People who are watching (e.g., a spouse, a coach, an ex-coach).
- The presence of someone who might be interested in inviting them to play or compete in the future.

Basically, their brains are occupied with everything but what they are supposed to be doing. All of this busy-ness occurs on the conscious level, and it's all so loud to them that we have to do a lot of work to get them to the point where their subconscious is able to block out all of the unimportant information that surrounds them. The human brain isn't designed to multi-task, and if you're attending to anything but what you're supposed to be doing, you're automatically at a disadvantage because you're putting your brain in a position where it must multi-task. And as you have likely experienced, you cannot do more than one thing well at once. Your athletic performance will suffer if you're thinking about anything other than the optimal way to behave and move in the moment you're in.

What is Concentration?

Concentration is the effortless ability to stay focused, and in the present, on the tasks that you need master in order to achieve your peak performance. We all have this ability, but most of us have difficulty concentrating consistently.

Excellent Concentration is Learned

Fortunately, if your concentration isn't great, you can improve it dramatically with some practice. (And a bonus of increasing your concentration is that your memory will improve, as well.) Hypnosis will unblock whatever is preventing your subconscious from maximum concentration. But just like with positive self-talk, relaxation and releasing performance anxiety, the best results occur when the power of hypnosis is bolstered by exercises you can do on the conscious level.

Concentration Busters

It's not that difficult for most people to lose their concentration; it doesn't take much. Here are the most common causes for loss of focus when you're competing:

1. Anxiety-perhaps you're concerned about the quality of your competition or your own readiness.
2. Lack of Confidence-When your confidence is low, too much mental energy is wasted on second-guessing your talents and abilities versus just moving well in the moment.
3. Distractions-Noises outside of you and inside your head are equally distracting.
4. Boredom-It can be easy to let your mind wander while you are engaged in an activity you've mastered on some level.

What Happens When Your Concentration is Lacking

When you aren't able to concentrate, your body tends to get stiff, and stiffness makes it difficult to feel what your body is doing as well as what your racket or club or bicycle is doing. Furthermore, your stomach and legs tighten. Once you're in this position, your hands and arms tighten up, further compromising anything you need to be doing with them. If you concentrate on being confident and relaxed, you'll be comfortable and able to perform.

Eliminating Potential Distractions is Impossible

The most effective way to improve your concentration is *not* to seek to eliminate distractions, but instead to change your relationship to them. In other words, you alter the way you experience the things, people, sounds and information around you. You choose to experience them as neutral, rather than disruptive. You acknowledge that they exist, and then forget about them. When you do this, your brain is able to focus better, as it's no longer drawn to sounds, sights and feelings that you ordinarily experience as distracting.

Luckily, there is one technique that can instantly help you with your concentration: attention, or rather, *attending* to something. You can be anywhere, doing anything, for this exercise. All you need is one word . . . or maybe two or three . . . Here are some versions of the attention exercise, and of changing your relationship to things you might experience as distractions:

Handling the noise inside your head

- Attend to your thoughts during the day, and when you
  notice them wandering, say to yourself: "concentrate," "be
  present," "be here now," or your own mantra if you already
  have one.
  The more attention you give to your thoughts, the more
  you'll realize that they wander around a lot during the day.
  Just remember that each time they wander, you can bring
  them back to the present and the task at hand.
- Reward yourself! When you've completed a task without
  having to use your mantra dozens of times, reward yourself.
  Praise yourself for your accomplishment.

Handling the noise outside your head

- While you are playing or working or doing whatever you
  need to concentrate on during the day, practice allowing
  whatever noises or movements that occur around you do so
  without looking at or reacting to them. Now, I'm not saying
  you should completely block out what's going on around
  you. This is about not being distracted by your surroundings,

but also being able to attend to anything you need to *despite* your surroundings. If you notice a sound or a movement, don't make a big deal out of noticing it; just move on to whatever you have to do.

- Reward yourself. When you've completed a task without attending to potential distractions in your surroundings, reward yourself. Praise yourself.

Advanced Concentration Exercise

- Sit in a comfortable chair in a quiet room where you won't be disturbed. Close your eyes and focus your attention on the space between your eyes. When you notice your attention moving away, notice where it went and bring it back.

- Repeat the exercise once again and have music with lyrics playing in the background. Is it harder to concentrate? Where does your mind go?

- If you can hold your attention on the space between your eyes for a full minute, you should have no problem concentrating on your event, regardless of outside distractions. If you think of a minute as a short amount of time, this exercise will give you a new perspective.

Focus isn't just a matter of inserting "concentration" into your subconscious. You have to work at broadening and deepening your awareness of what you're doing to subvert your focus, and do exercises to hone it, in addition to retraining your brain through hypnosis.

SANDY'S STORY

Sandy is a 15-year old girl who had been playing soccer for four years and was brought to me by her mother. Sandy's challenge was staying focused, concentrated and balanced. Her issue was one of performance anxiety. She was so anxious about not doing well that she wasn't able to perform well. She also had difficulty with players she didn't know (and their parents) watching her while she played. And of course that was most of the time. All of this was a lot for a 15-year old girl, and it kept her from playing as well as she could.

When she entered my office she was nervous and wanted to know what I was going to "do to" her. I explained and she was excited. She was very easily hypnotized and enjoyed it. We used the word "focus," and attached her focus on the task at hand to the word. We worked on "blanking out" the things and people she was experiencing as distracting.

When she returned for her next visit, she was so thrilled with how well it worked that she brought a list of things she wanted me to do for her. The second item on her list was that she wanted me to blank out her coach the way I had blanked out everyone else. And she said it was because the coach was always critical and that hurt her feelings. I told her that it wouldn't be professional for me to do that, but I could block out the hurt and the pain connected to what was said, and that would make her perform better.

Another thing on her list was that she would get so excited when she did well that she would miss whatever followed her excitement, which could have negative consequences for her and her teammates. I anchored in that she would be calm and relaxed after each shot she was in control over and ready for the next one.

Finally, we anchored in that every time she practiced or was on the field, no matter who was watching, all of the people were anchors for her to concentrate easier and better. She didn't even notice anyone was there.

Here's another common concentration problem . . .

DAN'S STORY

"My individual goals for now revolve around doing well and succeeding in swim competitions that involve backstroke. I've been swimming for my entire life and I have a natural talent for it. I know I'm good; that's not my problem. My problem is that I get so nervous before I begin a race that involves moving backwards that it prevents me from having the perfect performance that I know I'm capable of. I sometimes totally freeze when approaching the wall for my turn; that's the worst time. I forget my motions, even though I've gone over them thousands of times in my head and even physically practiced them!

"I experience feelings that are a lot like anxiety attacks. This problem creates devastating consequences for both me and my teammates. I've been very fortunate to have the ability to ignore my nervousness and just perform the way I was taught a lot of the time, but I'm not always that lucky. And when I'm not lucky, things get really bad. Disastrous, even. It's embarrassing for me to seem incapable of such a simple stroke and basically come unglued. It's nearly impossible for me to have fun if I can't get control of my nerves.

"My issues have snowballed from a few simple jitters into a condition that hinders everything about my performance. I fall apart because I don't have control over what occurs in my head while I'm swimming. And I honestly believe this is a psychological problem because I swim backstroke perfectly much of the time. But then, when I feel like everyone is watching me and judging me, I panic and begin to think about all of the things that can go wrong when I'm going backwards.

"When I swim backstroke, I know my mind isn't 100% concentrating on what I'm doing. Sometimes I don't even remember how it starts. It's like I'm distracted by something early on, but I still manage to compete. Before I know it, I'm imagining smashing my head against a wall and drowning and it's too late to recover and make decent time.

The Problem

Dan's language clearly indicates that his level of anxiety leads to a near-complete inability to concentrate while he's swimming backstroke.

The Solution

- Dan's first mission is to eliminate the thoughts of smashing his head and drowning by using the Release and Clear technique. Once his mind is no longer obsessing over negative thoughts, he'll be able to see possibilities and opportunities.
- Difficulties with concentration are often triggered by a specific place, such as the pool. Dan and I reframed his experience of the pool; I pointed out that he has plenty of feelings of safety and comfort and being able to concentrate when he's at the pool. We simply decided that regardless of what stroke he'd be swimming, he'd be equally comfortable and relaxed and prepared for peak athletic performance. In other words, we made the pool feel like home *all the time* to Dan, rather than just some of the time.
- To further alleviate Dan's anxiety and improve his ability to concentrate, I used an anchor to trigger Dan to slow down and breathe.

- I also used an anchor to connect the activity of approaching the wall to turn to feeling good and relaxing every time.
- I used Theater of the Mind to create a movie about Dan's new, desired behavior and performance. His mind will get accustomed to the perfect performance. It will be unable to distinguish that performance from reality, so it will then work to produce the performance.

The Result

"After four visits over two months, I swam backstroke in a meet for the first time. I felt a complete difference in my ability to concentrate. I noticed that it was like I was on autopilot just doing what I was supposed to do. I was focused and didn't hear all of the chatter that had been yelling in my head for so long, and my turns were perfect."

What to do now:

If you need to use Release and Clear to stop focusing on a negative experience from the past, do so after Instant Alpha Conditioning and before the *Gaining Concentration* script. If you don't need to Release and Clear, simply proceed to Instant Alpha and then to Gaining Concentration.

INSTANT ALPHA CONDITIONING

Instructions:

1) Use the word you selected to replace the Alpha conditioning technique introduced in *Calm, Cool, & Collected*. Read the following script and let Alpha occur.
2) Then proceed to the script for *Gaining Concentration*.

From this moment on, each and every time I desire to attain the deep state of total relaxation, I am instantly and fully relaxed, as I am now drifting into the Alpha state of consciousness. The moment I think my chosen word _____, Alpha occurs. This word has an effect only when I use it and only under the proper circumstances. Each and every time I do use it, I am fully prepared to receive positive, beneficial and constructive suggestions, impressing each one deeper into the storage and memory facility of my brain.

From this moment on, _____ triggers deep relaxation of my mind and body. I feel Alpha occur. I feel wonderful. I feel comfortable. I am totally receptive and responsive to my own creative ideas and suggestions. I am bathed in a glow of quietness, peace and serenity. My chosen word works only when I deliberately use it for deep relaxation to attain Alpha consciousness. Its use in regular conversation has no effect on me whatsoever. From this moment on, each and every time I desire the deep state of total relaxation, I am instantly and fully relaxed upon saying _____. Because my subconscious must follow my command, each and every time I desire total relaxation, I am instantly and fully relaxed when I think my chosen word_____. I feel a deep sense of gratification as this word programming becomes a reality. Feeling wonderful, generous, alive, and eager to Gain Concentration.

By regularly using the following hypnosis script, you'll be teaching your brain to block out all of the outside noises that prevent you from attending to the appropriate information. Retrain your brain to pay attention to your tasks at hand.

Gaining Concentration

I am totally focused and attentive when I practice as well as in competition. Just as a magnifying glass concentrates energy into a particular point of light, my mind excludes everything except the chosen task at hand. I am thankful for my ability to pay close attention to what my instructor is teaching . . . it's easy for me to concentrate. I am thankful for my ability to focus my faculties on a single purpose . . . I am thankful that I can concentrate on achieving my peak athletic performance.

I concentrate deeply and my ability to reason is strong. I know that I am a master of the art of concentration. I concentrate without effort. It's easy for me to focus and to keep my attention on my lesson, and also throughout my competitions. I exclude all else from my mind, while still being certain that my well-being is of the utmost importance.

I feel focused and attentive when I put on my uniform or dress for competition. I handle everything with confidence and self-assurance. It's so easy for me to concentrate . . . I easily learn new skills and conquer new challenges. Concentration opens doors to new areas for me . . . I am pleased that as I gain concentration, my capacity for learning and for development expands. I am attentive to details in all areas of my athletic experience. My ability to find a solution to a new challenge is rewarded with firmness of mind, and clarity of purpose. I persevere until I am satisfied with the outcome of my specific endeavor.

My ability to concentrate is strengthened each time I step onto the court or field or jump into the pool. Relaxation automatically increases my ability to concentrate. Concentration intensifies my mind and increases my awareness of my surroundings. I know that I desire to learn more . . . I solve whatever problems are before me. I become more relaxed and my concentration increases as my body's movement is as fluid as it can be.

My ability to concentrate reinforces all that I learn in my lessons. I am so thankful that my ability to concentrate expands my mind. My mind automatically executes what I successfully accomplish in my training. My mind is open and eager to use all of the knowledge that it gains.

I desire to concentrate thoroughly when I compete. I succeed admirably and I am pleased with my efforts. I am pleased with my ability to be attentive to details. My ability to find solutions to challenges is increased as I pay attention with firmness of mind and clarity of purpose. I persevere until I am satisfied with the outcome of my endeavors. The focus of my attention is strengthened each time I use my ability to concentrate, each time I grip a racket, each time I swing a club or take the field, and each time I cross a starting line.

The more I practice my sport, the more I master the art of concentration. Anytime I need assistance concentrating, I take a deep breath, exhale, and say the word "focus" quietly to myself. The word "focus" is a conditioned response key to my subconscious mind. When I say this word, I recapture my ability to concentrate.

This entire suggestion is represented by the letter "Y" of my sub-key word "RHYTHM." Anytime I think, say, or see the word "RHYTHM," all suggestions keyed to this word are automatically activated, stimulated, and work for my benefit.

You now have the choice to either awaken or to drift off into a normal, natural sleep. If you are going to awaken, say:

Twenty minutes. Wide awake.

If you are going to drift off into a normal, natural sleep, say:

I am now going to drift off into a normal, natural sleep. When I awaken, I will feel fully rested, calm, and at peace with myself, the world and those around me.

CHAPTER 7

KEY #4
RELEASE OF
PERFORMANCE ANXIETY
YOUR EMOTIONAL STATE: FROM
APPREHENSIVE TO ASSURED

WHEN you first learned how to ride a bicycle, you probably had a good dose of performance anxiety. There you were, with your mother watching and your father holding the seat and the handlebars, walking along side you. You knew that your father was going to let go soon and you'd be riding *all by yourself*. If you were like most people, you were thinking of everything you had to do: balance, peddle, steer, and sit up straight. Oh, and breathe and keep your eyes open.

That's an awful lot to think about, especially when your entire family is watching you. Your heart pounds, you think and think and think about all of the physical movements you have to keep track of, and you're so nervous and so hyper-aware that you actually recall having to send a signal from your brain to your feet to start peddling.

That's performance anxiety.

Now, fast forward one year, and picture yourself whizzing around the neighborhood, doing the slalom around the trees, hopping over curbs and doing wheelies. You're in "the zone." The only thing you're thinking about is beating your own record for speeding down the street. Your feet pedal as fast as they can, but know when to stop for an upcoming jump. Your arms pull the handlebars up exactly at the right time, and you effortlessly lift your entire body—and your bike—a foot in the air to hop a large curb. You aren't conscious of any of this, yet it all happens.

That's "the zone." Peak performance, flow, the zone, your best performance . . . they all mean the same thing. You have no awareness of time or space, your focus is razor-sharp, and your movements are fluid and spontaneous. And you're happy.

Hypnosis is a very important part of releasing performance anxiety, as it turns the anxiety switch from "on" to "off." But hypnosis doesn't solve the problem completely. There is a lot of work you should do with your conscious self to help you relieve some of the physical and mental tension you experience about your upcoming performances. First I'll give you some tips and practical exercises . . .

- **Be prepared.**
  No amount of hypnosis is going to help you if you aren't prepared to do your best. This includes practicing under conditions that are similar to what you'll experience during your game, meet, race, or other competition. Eat right, sleep well, exercise, do some deep breathing or meditating. Just as athletes regularly train their bodies to execute precise skills or maintain a certain pace, they need to regularly train their minds to think precise thoughts and focus on specific things.

- **Don't expect perfection.**

  Athletes train their physical skills for years, trying to achieve the perfect performance. I think I've seen perfect performances, but I sure wouldn't want to strive for perfection. As I've discussed previously, perfection assumes that there's always another level, and another level, and another level that you can reach. Just the notion of it is exhausting and debilitating to many people mentally, as they presumably will always strive for it and never reach it.

  When preparing for a competition, you give yourself hundreds, maybe even thousands, of suggestions. If your thoughts during this time are confident and positive, your mind and body respond well, and you can enjoy great performance. If your thoughts are concerned with pressuring yourself to execute the perfect performance, the stress of that unreasonable expectation will prevent you from enjoying yourself and hamper your performance.

- **Control your environment.**

  You can't control everything, but you can control whom you spend time with and how you react to them. If there's someone in your life who pushes all your buttons, either don't spend time with that person, or change the way you react to them and their behavior. (The latter is possible, but takes time. The former is a quicker, easier fix, but also can be viewed as cosmetic, as it doesn't actually get to the core of the problem.)

- **Relax.**

  It's difficult when your attempts at relaxation are solely on a conscious level. Use the exercises in *Calm, Cool, & Collected* to help you alleviate some of the physical and emotional stress you feel when you're full of anxiety. And the script from that chapter uses the subconscious to create relaxation that's deeper and more immediate than you'll be able to achieve on the conscious level.

- **Empower yourself with self-talk.**
  Assume success, imagine success, and you'll get it, providing you've done what you need to do to prepare for it.

- **Make your mistakes work for you.**
  Remember that *mistakes are just feedback*. A mistake simply tells you that there's something you need to do differently. You might not immediately know what you need to do differently, but you can start experimenting as soon as you've received feedback: an outcome that you didn't want. Once you've recognized that you're making a mistake, you must make a commitment to not reproducing that mistake: a commitment to turn it around. What's crucial here is the desire to change. If you have no desire to change, you simply will not be able to. Therefore, ask yourself the question: "Do I really want to change behavior X?" If the answer is yes, make a conscious commitment to make your mistakes work *for* you, not against you. We'll be delving more into mistakes in Key #6, but for now, think about changing your relationship to them (like you're working on changing your relationship to the things in your surroundings that you might call distractions), and seeing them as useful information.

- **Be patient.**

  It has taken months, or even years, for you to develop the pattern of mistakes that you are currently making. Once you've made a commitment to change your mistakes to work for you, stick with that commitment. Don't give up. Everyone is different. Some athletes may be able to fix their mistakes and turn them around by doing at-home sessions and exercises once a week. Others may need to listen to a self-hypnosis CD for 21 sessions a month. Yet other athletes may need to enlist the assistance of a live hypnotist to help them overcome their fears, negative self-talk, or other self-inflicted ailments.

  Here are some exercises you can do to help alleviate your performance anxiety:

- **Imagine peak performance.**

  This is basically positive visualization. Imagine yourself giving the optimal performance. Create a complete, rich sensory experience. For example, if your sport is baseball, imagine what you look like, what your glove looks like, how the bat feels in your hands, the perfect tempo of your swing, what you smell, and what you hear. The more detailed your image is, the better. Note that imagining peak performance and expecting perfection are *not* the same thing. And on the field, remember that your brain doesn't know the difference between your memory of something real and something you have imagined. Imagining doesn't have the pressure and emotion attached to it that *expectation* has. Expectation can lead to disappointment; imagination cannot. This type of visualization is entirely from your perspective: how you feel, what you see, what you are thinking, and what ultimately happens.

The flipside of visualizing how you feel is to picture yourself as a third party. Watch a movie of yourself on the field playing. This is Theater of the Mind. For example, let's say you're a golfer. Find a quiet place and visualize yourself playing in a tournament, executing a gorgeous swing and making eagles left and right. You're a spectator here this time, and you can use your imagination to create anything. What do you look like? What is around you? Pan around with your mental camera. Zoom in for a close-up on your face. What would you have to be thinking and feeling in order to look like your close up? Create those thoughts and feelings the next time you play golf.

- **Thought awareness.**
  Observe your thoughts as they run through your head. Don't try to stop or edit them—just let them go. Make a mental note of how many times, and to what degree, you worry, dwell on negatives, criticize yourself, think of something anxiety-provoking, or think of yourself as inadequate or a failure. Awareness is the first step toward developing positive thinking.

  A great way to demonstrate to yourself just how absurd some of your thoughts are is to put them on paper. Write down negative thoughts as soon as they occur. You'll probably get a good laugh at some of the stuff that comes into your head, but once the amusement ends, you've got to get down to the business of making a change in your thought process.

- **Negative-thought stopping.**

  Remember that your thoughts create your reality; they create physical reactions. Negative self-talk is destructive to your growth as an athlete and a competitor. This seemingly simple exercise consists of four steps: (1) Become aware of the negative self-talk; (2) Stop the negative talk as soon as it occurs; (3) Replace the negative talk with positive talk; and (4) Repeat and practice this exercise as often as negative thoughts enter your mind.

  Utilize the power of positive speech to erase negative thoughts from your vocabulary. At first, it won't be easy to erase the negative thoughts. Not only is your mind not used to having its thoughts interrupted, but also it will automatically fight the acceptance of the positive thought, *merely because it is different; it's not what your mind is accustomed to.* The only way to change this is through persistence and repetition. *Practice.* Make negative-thought stopping part of your daily routine.

- **Cultivate positive thinking.**

  I'm referring to more than replacing your negative thoughts with positive ones, here. Cultivating positive thinking means creating a habit of optimism through affirmations and changing the way you use language on a day-to-day basis. It means striving to see the good in people rather than instantly recognizing the bad and focusing on it. It means creating positive habits, such as saying "please" and "thank you" and being compassionate and kind to the woman who checks out your groceries or waits on you at lunch, or the gentleman who picks up your garbage.

- **Model an athlete you admire.**

  The athlete may be someone famous, or may be a friend
  of yours whose talents and skills you would like to
  emulate. Again, find a quiet place, perhaps in the locker
  room or at home, and visualize your face and body with that
  person's balanced and confident athletic performance. Your
  intention is to observe another as if they were you. This
  particular technique is more advanced and takes more practice than the previous ones. I suggest that you practice them
  first before moving on to this technique.

  You will find that visualization is a comforting and peaceful
  experience. It has a calming affect upon you both mentally
  and physically. Your heart rate slows and you feel a renewed
  sense of confidence.

- **Breathe.**

  For immediate relief when you find yourself in a circumstance that makes you nervous or anxious, focus on your
  breath. Take slow, deep breaths. When we're nervous, our
  breath is immediately affected. It either becomes very quick
  and shallow, or it comes to a virtual stop. And your brain
  needs oxygen and uses 25% of the oxygen you breathe, so
  if you're not breathing, you're putting your brain at a disadvantage. By concentrating on taking slow, deep, methodical
  breaths, you: 1) Take your mind off of the immediate situation that is making you nervous; 2) Bring necessary oxygen
  to your organs and muscles, which will help you physically
  relax; and 3) Slow your heart rate down so it's no longer
  racing. You can practice this exercise anywhere and any time.
  It's easy, inconspicuous, and fast acting.

- **Anchoring.**

  As you know by now, anchors are commonly used in self-hypnosis and hypnosis to reinforce positive self-talk. Examples of anchors that you should be familiar with by now are gripping a racket, holding a ball, and putting on running shoes. You can create your own anchors for use in the customized self-hypnosis scripts you'll be writing later. You can even start using anchors today, before you go to sleep. For example, if you have a bicycle race tomorrow morning, maybe you'll choose touching the handlebars as your anchor. While you're lying on your bed, relaxing and breathing deeply this evening, simply say to yourself: "The moment I touch my handlebars, I feel instantly calm and relaxed . . . The moment I touch my handlebars, I feel instantly calm and relaxed . . . The moment I touch my handlebars, I feel instantly calm and relaxed."
  Maybe your anchor will be the touching of your visor or your sweatband. You may even choose a color as an anchor. Regardless, make sure that you choose an anchor that's simple to use and uncomplicated to access.

- **Forgive yourself.**

  If and when you make a mistake, even after utilizing techniques to eliminate your mistakes, you must learn how to forgive yourself. You're human and humans make mistakes. You're not infallible; you're not perfect. The best athletes in the world and the most accomplished players make mistakes. Remember that it's how you choose to handle mistakes that's essential to your ability to make progress. Rather than counting your mistakes, learn from them

and be thankful for the opportunity to learn. Remember,
they're only feedback.

- **Use affirmations.**
  Create first person affirmations for yourself and read them
  to yourself, both silently and out loud, in the privacy of
  your own home or office. Depending on your own personal
  needs, you may want to read them once or twice a day, just
  a couple of days before a match, meet, or a game, or all
  day long during the times that you're playing in a tournament. The more often you read them, the more intense the
  affirmations will become. Read them like you mean it. Don't
  just mindlessly read the words. Focus on each sentence as
  you read, and don't let yourself be distracted by outside
  noises or events.
  Create affirmations that are personal to you and your
  specific situation or circumstance. Make sure to eliminate
  any negative talk and clearly state the outcome you want as
  if it has already occurred—not that it will (you hope . . . you
  wish . . . you pray) occur. Write your affirmations neatly on
  large pieces of paper so that the words are easy to see and
  repeat. You can even laminate them to ensure that they are
  preserved and protected from the wear and tear of everyday
  use. Place a copy of your laminated affirmations in your
  sports bag to ensure that it is always there for inspiration.
  Place a laminated one in your shower.

- **List your mistakes.**
  Everyone should write out their goals. Your list should
  include a description of what you call mistakes (which are
  really just information, remember), a personal statement by

you about how you will accomplish your goal, and part of that is by turning your "mistake" into positive action that will prevent it from recurring. In my Solutions program, I would have you write two lists. The first one has your mistakes and problems, and the second has your solutions and a timetable for your actions. Once the second list is written, you physically tear up and throw away (or even burn—safely) the first one.

- **Confide in a friend.**
  It's unhealthy to keep negative thoughts and fears inside. Confiding in a friend is a healthy way to vent, as long as you choose your listener carefully (i.e., make sure the person is ready to listen).

- **Get expert help.**
  Enlist the help of experts to assist you in making your mistakes work for you. Find a skilled hypntist to visit. Make sure to check out their credentials. You can tell if the person is a skilled professional. Look for the initials "CHt or CH" after their name for "certified hypnotist." Ask the professional where they studied and who they studied under. Feel free to ask them for references. If the person is a true professional, they should be more than willing to give you such information to confirm their legitimacy.

CAITLIN'S STORY

"I often think that I'm not a good enough player to be playing at the courts. It seems like all of the other players are so tall, poised and polished. I swear that the other players look perfect, and that

I just don't fit in. Plus, I am scared to play with them because they all have better returns than me. Whenever they ask me to play, I always tell them that I have a scheduling conflict, even if I don't. There's just no way that I will be able to compete against players who are better than I am and who even look like they are better than me. I decided that I needed to improve my personal thoughts about myself. To learn how to like myself. Since I've always been put down by my parents and my sister and brothers, it's really hard for me to think I can do anything right. It seems that growing up the harder I tried to be perfect, the more I was put down. This has affected every aspect of my life. I obviously hadn't made any headway dealing with this on my own, so I decided to get help."

After three sessions of hypnosis and two weeks of listening to the Release of Performance Anxiety CD. . .

"I'm finally moving forward and have played successful matches. I've discovered that I'm a wonderful person and I even have talent. And I have a lot to share with other people. There's no reason why I can't hit tennis shots just as well, if not better than everyone else. During my sessions with Laura, I learned about the difference between perfectionism and being perfect. I learned that by constantly driving myself to perfection, I was practically guaranteeing that everything I was doing wasn't going to be good enough. Once I came to the realization that at any given moment I am perfect in that moment and that everything else I do is in preparation of being perfect within the next moment, I started to feel so much lighter—like the weight of all of my anxiety was being lifted. Now I just go into that wonderful zone where I'm on autopilot, and I play well."

INSTANT ALPHA CONDITIONING

Instructions:

1) Use the word you selected to replace the Alpha conditioning technique introduced in *Calm, Cool, & Collected*. Read the following script and let Alpha occur.
2) Then proceed to the script for *Release of Performance Anxiety*.

From this moment on, each and every time I desire to attain the deep state of total relaxation, I am instantly and fully relaxed, as I am now drifting into the Alpha state of consciousness. The moment I think my chosen word _____, Alpha occurs. This word has an effect only when I use it and only under the proper circumstances. Each and every time I do use it, I am fully prepared to receive positive, beneficial and constructive suggestions, impressing each one deeper into the storage and memory facility of my brain.

From this moment on, _____ triggers deep relaxation of my mind and body. I feel Alpha occur. I feel wonderful. I feel comfortable. I am totally receptive and responsive to my own creative ideas and suggestions. I am bathed in a glow of quietness, peace and serenity. My chosen word works only when I deliberately use it for deep relaxation to attain Alpha consciousness. Its use in regular conversation has no effect on me whatsoever. From this moment on, each and every time I desire the deep state of total relaxation, I am instantly and fully relaxed upon saying _____. Because my subconscious must follow my command, each and every time I desire total relaxation, I am instantly and fully relaxed when I think my chosen word_____. I feel a deep sense of gratification as this word programming becomes a reality. Feeling wonderful, generous, alive and eager to Release Performance Anxiety.

RELEASE OF PERFORMANCE ANXIETY

I enjoy playing my sport . . . I enjoy performing in front of others. I am self-reliant and comfortable being a winner when I perform. I release all performance anxiety I have ever experienced in the past . . . I release everything negative connected with those experiences. I am free from any fears of performance anxiety . . . free to be me. I accept myself completely . . . I love myself.

When I picture myself before a group of spectators, I take in a deep breath and then exhale completely. This makes me relaxed and centered inside. I smile and feel at ease as I imagine myself performing in front of others. I am confident in my ability to be calm. I smile at the prospect of performing well in front of others.

I am thankful for the opportunity to participate in my sport. I enjoy practicing and competing, testing my own talents and abilities. When I am in competition, my mind is occupied only with the task at hand. I know that I am skilled … I know that I am talented. I am well prepared to meet my goals. I give each movement my full attention. It's easy for me to focus and I execute every movement, no matter how complex, with confidence and precision.

I am a winner . . . I enjoy competing to test my abilities . . . My attitude is positive and full of fun . . . I focus my attention on the task at hand . . . I keep my concentration as long as I want to . . . I am decisive and make correct decisions easily . . . I am consistent because I am focused . . . my body and mind are in perfect harmony . . . I give my performance my full intention and attention. I am proud of myself . . . I behave like a winner . . . I have all the traits of a winner

. . . I know that I deserve peak performance. I know that I deserve to win. I am a true competitor and athlete.

If a performance doesn't come off as planned, I deal with any mistakes in a calm and effective manner. I take any mistakes that may occur in stride. I do not accept negative thoughts or feelings. I handle all situations easily and effectively, which separates me from the other athletes. I am thankful that I meet any challenge before me with ease. I am ready for any challenge. I compete with confidence and poise.

I am a winner. Success moves throughout my entire body and makes me feel wonderful. I give each performance 100% of my attention. Each successful challenge that I conquer is imprinted on my subconscious mind as a blueprint that is recalled at any moment in time. My mind applies this blueprint to my mind/body connection so that my muscle memory is always there for me to achieve peak performance.

I enjoy competing in front of others because I enjoy sharing my skills and talents with other people. I enjoy being successful . . . I feel like a winner through and through. I am secure and confident. Positive radiance shines from me.

Every time I want to relax before I compete, I ("hold my racket," "touch my swimsuit," "grip my club," etc.) and repeat the word "relax" silently to myself. "Relax" . . . "relax." I take a deep breath in and then exhale . . . "relax." The energy of being a winner surges throughout my entire body. I feel at ease and in total control. I am confident and calm with my competition skills. This inner warmth that I feel grants me happiness and success.

This special cue of ("holding my racket," "touching my swimsuit," "gripping my club," etc.) and saying the word "relax" to myself always works for me in this way. Whenever I need to relax and release any performance anxiety, I ("hold my racket," "touch my swimsuit," "grip my club," etc.) and say the word "relax" silently to myself. My body feels wonderful, powerful, focused and in control.

This entire suggestion is represented by the letter "T" of my sub-key word "RHYTHM." Anytime I think, say, or see the word "RHYTHM," all suggestions keyed to this word are automatically activated, stimulated and work for my benefit.

You now have the choice to either awaken or to drift off into a normal, natural sleep. If you are going to awaken, say:

Twenty minutes. Wide awake.

If you are going to drift off into a normal, natural sleep, say:

I am now going to drift off into a normal, natural sleep. When I awaken, I will feel fully rested, calm, and at peace with myself, the world and those around me.

CHAPTER 8

KEY #5
MASTERING FEAR
YOUR MENTAL STATE: FROM TERRIFIED TO INTREPID

Fear makes the wolf bigger than he is.

German proverb

What is your biggest fear when competing?
Are there people around you who feed your fears?
How do you feel when you are around them?
How many times a day do you feel fearful?
Is there a payoff to feeling fearful?
Is there a cost to feeling fearful?
Does fear affect your decision-making?
What are you attached to? (e.g., are you fearful of losing?)
Where does your fear show up?

REGARDLESS of your particular fear profile, your fears hold you back from achieving peak performance and from feeling happiness, self-worth, and inner peace. In this chapter, I'll examine what fear is and how it affects you mentally and physically and I'll discuss what you can do—today—to rid yourself of the fears that are keeping you from becoming the athlete you can be.

What is fear?

Fear is a painful emotion triggered by the apprehension of (real or imagined) danger, terror, or displeasure. I say real or imagined because many of our fears are merely concoctions of our imagination. But as I have discussed many times, your subconscious mind cannot distinguish between real images and imagined fears; it will produce the same fear response throughout the body for both. And then, as you probably know by now, what you fear is then likely to become your reality.

Some fear is not just imagined—but irrational!

I'm sure you've heard many times that the most common fear is of public speaking. It's more common than the fear of death (which, in case you were wondering, weighs in at #7). This is a perfect example of how irrational fear can be. Let's say you are indeed afraid of public speaking. What exactly is it that you are afraid of? Is public speaking a life and death situation for you? For *anyone?* Are you even likely to be physically hurt in any way as a result of public speaking, even if you are terrible at it?

No.

Fear is your mind's way of making a potentially embarrassing or uncomfortable situation seem more threatening than it really is. Essentially, fear makes mountains out of molehills and prevents us from enjoying our lives, our playing, and the calculated risks we take. You may have even heard FEAR defined as False Evidence Appearing Real.

How does fear affect you physically?

Once the brain gets the signal that there is something to fear (whether or not there is, in reality), it releases hormones throughout the body that trigger defensive chemical mechanisms. This is the "fight or flight" response we've all heard about and experienced.

Here's what happens:

- In the first fraction of a second, the brain tells the adrenal glands to produce and release adrenalin (epinephrine) into the bloodstream.
- Within seconds, adrenaline rushes through you.
- Your heart races, your digestion slows and your blood pressure rises. You're prepared for a potentially life-changing decision: whether to remain and fight whatever threatens you, or flee.
- If whatever was stressing you is still present, your brain tells your adrenals to produce and secrete the stress hormone cortisol, which gives you a quick burst of energy and strength (because there is increased blood flow to your extremities), and a lower sensitivity to pain.
- Ideally, within minutes, whatever you felt threatened by goes away or is handled, and your body returns to a state of relaxation.

Your body will go into the same full-blown fight-or-flight response when you're beginning a game or competition as it does when you are jumping out of a plane or off a cliff.

And then . . .

Burnout Can Occur

The fight-or-flight mechanism isn't meant to be triggered multiple times in a short period of time. As you may have noticed, when it *is* triggered, you usually experience the physical cues as stress, as *you do rationally know that your life is not in danger.* But stress after stress eventually leads to exhaustion and burnout because your adrenals continuously pump out adrenalin and cortisol, and your body and your mind don't ever get to return to the state of relaxation. Chronic stress and prolonged levels of cortisol in the bloodstream diminishes all of your capacities and creates problems such as:

- sleep challenges
- fatigue
- weight gain (stress drives you to eat and cortisol makes you crave readily available sources of energy, such as high fat, simple carbohydrate foods, and it also encourages your body to store fat for survival)
- digestive issues
- headaches
- nervousness
- problems with coordination

Conquering Fear

Fearless: calmly resolute in facing real or imagined dangers or perils.
Freedom from fear.

To overcome your fear, you must first identify where and when you learned it. Is it rational? Irrational? Either way, it is real to you in your mind, and sometimes once you acknowledge the origin as irrational, it becomes easier to overcome.

Consider this . . .

The changeover from swimming to cycling during triathlons has always been easy for Shannon. But transitioning from cycling to running has always been difficult. She has lost time, injured herself, and often blames her "disastrous times" on her inefficiency/lack of success with that transition. In fact, she has yet to have what she would call a successful changeover to running, so in her mind she has no reason to believe she can ever have one. Meanwhile, during practice, her transitions are fine, so mentally she is perfectly aware that she is capable of doing them efficiently and swiftly. Because of the level of disappointment Shannon has experienced in competition, however ("when it matters," as she says), she has paralyzing fear of that changeover and her results have been pretty bad. That's the bad news. But the good news is that she knows that this situation is all in her head because she does so well during practice. She knows that fear is her problem.

You have two choices with your fears: face them or be paralyzed by them. Shannon spent some time being paralyzed, as most people do, but then decided to take action. She believed in her ability to change her fear and was resolute that it wasn't going to control her any longer. And that was half the battle.

Shannon wrote a *fear profile;* it's the history—the biography— of your fear. Frankly, once Shannon saw her fear profile in writing, she immediately overcame it consciously, as her particular fear, though understandable and common, wasn't all that rational. What was going through her mind was that she was afraid "messing up" her changeovers like she had in the past, so she kept reliving those changeovers. Meanwhile, she had perfectly efficient changeovers during practice, so she already had visions of herself executing them fabulously but she wasn't using those visions, those visualizations. She was using the wrong ones (and yes, for good reason, as the ones she was using were the ones that actually counted).

Whether your fear is of a past experience recurring or of something new (e.g., fear of the unknown, fear of a certain type of hit, or competing on a new surface or in a new place), that fear tends to be relived over and over again until it has snowballed to such a point that it is all-consuming.

You might think that I am going to help you eliminate your fear, but actually there is no such thing. Instead, we aim for mastery of the fear. As Mark Twain once said, *"Courage is resistance to and mastery of fear—not the absence of fear."* In order to master your fear, you must identify it and get to know it well.

EXERCISES TO HELP YOU MASTER YOUR FEARS

- **Write your *fear profile*.**
  Everyone should begin here and do this exercise at least once with each fear. Give your fear a name and write its biography. When did it come into your life? Why? Describe the day, if you recall, and/or the circumstance. Like when you are doing a Theater of the Mind exercise, compose a story with rich sensory details. Often the mere creation and writing of the story deepens your understanding of your fear and helps you master it. Remember, you cannot master something if you don't know it well.

- **Instant change of state.**
  The instant an unpleasant thought enters your mind, simply

assure yourself that "The most powerful experience of this moment is the relaxation I am feeling." When you say this, you are diminishing the power of the fear and its effect on you. You are taken to a place of safety and serenity so your body can use its precious resources on focusing on your performance rather on overreacting.

Face your fears slowly to desensitize yourself to their effects. And repeat your exposure to them over and over again until you realize that the dread in your head is much greater than the actual potential for harm.

- **Breathwork.**
  The in-breath followed by the out-breath represents tension and release. And when the breath is blocked, the body and mind are blocked and in a state of substandard performance. There must be freely flowing breath in order for there to be peak performance. When you disconnect from your breath, you prevent flow, you get lost on your way to the zone.

- **Blowing your fears away.**
  Find a quiet place and breathe deeply, slowly and completely. Visualize the thing, event, or person that is at the center of your biggest fear. See everything about the moment you fear most, and then add more sensory details. Feel that moment of your biggest fear. Smell it. Hear it.

Then . . .

Shrink it.

Continue to shrink the picture in your mind until it is so small that when you hold it in the palm of your hand you can barely see, feel, smell, or hear it.

Then . . .
Blow on it once, and send it off into oblivion, never to return.

SELF-HYPNOSIS FOR *MASTERING FEAR*

INSTANT ALPHA CONDITIONING

Instructions:

1) Use the word you selected to replace the Alpha conditioning technique introduced in *Calm, Cool, & Collected*. Read the following script and let Alpha occur.
2) Then proceed to the script for *Mastering Fear*.

From this moment on, each and every time I desire to attain the deep state of total relaxation, I am instantly and fully relaxed, as I am now drifting into the Alpha state of consciousness. The moment I think my chosen word _____, Alpha occurs. This word has an effect only when I use it and only under the proper circumstances. Each and every time I do use it, I am fully prepared to receive positive, beneficial and constructive suggestions, impressing each one deeper into the storage and memory facility of my brain.

From this moment on, _____ triggers deep relaxation of my mind and body. I feel Alpha occur. I feel wonderful. I feel comfortable. I am totally receptive and responsive to my own creative ideas and suggestions. I am bathed in a glow of quietness, peace and serenity. My chosen word works only when I deliberately use it for deep relaxation to attain Alpha consciousness. Its use in regular conversation has no effect on me whatsoever. From this moment on, each and every time I desire the deep state of total relaxation, I am instantly and fully relaxed upon saying _____. Because my subconscious must follow my command, each and every time I desire total relaxation, I am instantly and fully relaxed when I think my chosen word_____. I feel a deep sense of gratification as this word programming becomes a reality. Feeling wonderful, generous, alive and eager to Master My Fears.

MASTERING FEAR

I am self-assured and confident in my ability to compete. I use positive and empowering self-talk to achieve my goals. I am in control of my life. I no longer have fear-based emotions. I relax and release every fearful experience of the past and everything connected with those experiences. It is so easy to let go of my fears. My positive experiences supply me with the energy to meet all the challenges that I encounter when I'm engaged in practice and in competition. My subconscious mind has the amazing ability to disengage from every negative and harmful impression ever made upon me.

I am grateful and thankful for every experience of the past. I forgive myself for every mistake I have ever made, and I forgive everyone else who may have in any way harmed me. I know that good comes out of each experience. I grow stronger with each and every experience . . . I am stronger than anything life can offer. I am prepared to meet any competition challenge that I encounter in a state of mind that is free from negative thoughts. I possess the power and the ability to channel any occurrence into a rich and rewarding experience.

I am open to new suggestions, which I accept and act upon. I am open to all the warmth, joy and fulfillment that being an athlete has to offer. I feel glad to be alive and enthusiastic about my future. I am thankful that I have the opportunity to compete. I am calm and relaxed and a sense of peace permeates my body and mind. I fully release the past fears and all the effects that these fears have had upon me. I am free . . . free of the past fears related to my athletic performance . . . free to be me entirely. I accept myself completely . . . I am a valuable and talented human being . . . I am always aware of my innate worth. There are things that I do that are done better by me than by any other human being. There is no one who can exactly duplicate me . . . I accept myself . . . I love myself. I am grateful for my new level of understanding.

I easily visualize myself in competition. I love the powerful feeling that it gives me. I enjoy the harmony and balance of entire body as it moves exactly the way it should for my optimal performance . . . I thoroughly enjoy the way mind feels, too. I am confident and poised and I'm proud of that.

In order to prepare to compete, I go through what I need to do quietly in my mind. My mind is serene as I take slow, deep breaths and allow quiet to occupy my insides . . . I spend several minutes going over what I need to do in my mind . . . I relax and breathe . . . relax and breathe . . . relax and breathe. I'm calm and I trust that all is right. If there are any unnecessary internal voices, I use counting so that my unconscious mind can assume control of my body and its reactions. Ten . . . relax, nine . . . breathe . . . eight, relax, seven, six . . . breathe . . . five, four . . . breathe . . . three, relax . . . two . . . one. Counting calmly puts me into a state of relaxation. I feel composed and free of tension. My breathing is slow and even.

I become totally immersed in the experience of competing. The fluid and graceful tempo of my body, and the peace of my mind are what I expect and what I experience. I physically anchor the calm and wonderful feeling of competition by ("holding my racket," "touching my swimsuit," "gripping my club," etc.). This is my trigger that anchors these pleasant feelings of calm and confidence as I compete. I am confident, calm and relaxed every time I ("hold my racket," "touch my swimsuit," "grip my club," etc.).

It is calming for me to picture in my mind the successful completion of my event. It's easy for me to prepare my mind by simply going through my routine mentally – I visualize my performance and this makes me calm. I am completely certain about what I am about to do. I breathe deeply to relax my mind and body before I start. I become perfectly comfortable as I continue my performance, all the way through until the end. My performance is magnificent and I am so pleased, yet calm.

I feel self assured, light, supple, poised, composed and confident at the prospect of my success. I ("hold my racket," "touch my swimsuit," "grip my club," etc.) and play with rhythm, tempo, balance and harmony.

I am balanced and in harmony as I finish with calm, confidence and poise. Counting to myself makes me more relaxed and I remember to breathe calmly and slowly. I finish feeling confident, and I leave my event feeling better than I have ever felt in my whole life. I perform up to my maximum potential and I listen to my body's limitations and warning signals. I ("hold my racket," "touch my swimsuit," "grip my club," etc.) as my anchor to promote feelings of calm and confidence.

This entire suggestion is represented by the letter "H" of my sub-key word "RHYTHM." Anytime I think, say, or see the word "RHYTHM," all suggestions keyed to this word are automatically activated, stimulated and work for my benefit.

You now have the choice to either awaken or to drift off into a normal, natural sleep. If you are going to awaken, say:

Twenty minutes. Wide awake.

If you are going to drift off into a normal, natural sleep, say:

I am now going to drift off into a normal, natural sleep. When I awaken, I will feel fully rested, calm, and at peace with myself, the world and those around me.

CHAPTER 9

KEY #6
ACHIEVING PEAK PERFORMANCE
YOUR EXPECTATIONS: FROM AWFUL TO AWESOME

Your attitude toward defeat is crucial to mastering it. You can see it only as a loss or as a chance for gain.

Napoleon Hill, *Keys to Success:*
The 17 Principles of Personal Achievement

D O you condemn yourself for things that you did in the past? Don't worry, everyone does at some point. Perhaps there are choices you made at crucial turning points in your life that you'd like to take back. Maybe you treated someone you cared for poorly and wish you had another chance. In your athletic history, perhaps you made a mistake that cost you a game or a point or a race, and you're still angry and frustrated with yourself about it.

If you want to be successful at any athletic endeavor, as well as life in general, it's crucial that you release the past and not blame yourself for events that have already transpired and that you cannot change.

Ask yourself this question: Has beating yourself up about the past ever helped you or made you feel better? Has it ever improved your athletic performance? If your answer is no, this chapter is tailor made for you!

This chapter will approach peak performance from the inside out by helping you eliminate the self-defeating behavior involved in clinging to mistakes of the past.

Choosing to Change is Not Enough

Changing your behavior is more than just making the decision to do it. A perfect example is what most people do with New Year's resolutions. Once a year, with enthusiasm and confidence, many people proclaim: "This year, I'm going to be a more positive person," or, "This is the year I'm going to treat my body better and lose those 20 pounds." They claim that acknowledging that they need to change is the first step toward achieving their goals. And that's true.

But by February 1, most New Year's resolutions are distant memories, and precious little progress has been made toward goals that were supposed to be of the utmost importance.

Going to Seminars and Buying CDs is Not Enough

For many people, once they realize that they need some help to get over their past mistakes and achieve what they are capable of, they go to a seminar and/or order some self-help CDs. They jump up and down, clap, and cheer enthusiastically at the seminar, then listen to the CDs every day for a week or two. Soon the excitement of their personal potential wears off and, well, they're back to where they started.

What's Missing? What's the Secret Ingredient?

Actually, there are two secret ingredients, and they work together: using the subconscious to deliver your goals, and practicing your desired physical behavior (i.e., your swing, your changeover, etc.) and your desired mental behavior (i.e., your thought patterns). After all, what keeps many people from accomplishing their goals can usually be distilled down to one simple concept: their behavior doesn't support their goal.

What do you do if your coach teaches you how to pitch a better softball? You practice it until you get it right, of course. What eludes most people is that changing the way we approach our thoughts should be handled the same way. So if you feel like you beat yourself up over past mistakes and you want to change that thought-behavior, you'll be much more successful if you practice, practice, practice.

Fortunately, peak performance is a learned ability. It's reached on a consistent basis because of training. Not luck, not talent, and not just practice. Over time, you can move from however you are feeling and performing in a particular moment, to how you *need* to feel at that moment.

The successful person recommends this approach: If you've done something in the past that you feel you can and should change, then by all means take action. If you've been unkind to someone, apologize to them. If you failed to fulfill a promise you made, take steps to fulfill that promise. If you made a mistake on the playing field, devote more of your practice time to whatever it was you had difficulty with.

The unsuccessful person wallows in regret and self-pity over these things and uses language that furthers the depth of their misery. Naturally, the unsuccessful person is then unable to move forward. The strategy of berating yourself for past conduct solves nothing and serves only to lower your self-esteem. You create a vicious cycle where negative experiences and negative feelings are reinforced, which leads to more negative outcomes and more negative feelings. You aren't going to change one bit of your past. What's done is done. Learn from your past experiences and move on. You did the best you could, given your awareness and understanding of your options at the time. You are human and it's in our nature to make mistakes. You have nothing to gain from self-condemnation except feelings of misery and inadequacy.

Below are the Top 10 Mistakes Athletes Make. I'm sure you'll find a couple—if not all—of your mistakes in the list.

TOP 10 MISTAKES ATHLETES MAKE

10. Imagining failure.
    If you visualize missing the return, hitting the ball into the water, not having a fluid stroke, messing up a changeover or throwing an interception. . . Guess what's going to happen?

9. Playing nervously.
    Your body responds to your nerves, which causes you to hold your breath. Without your breathing you're tense because you cannot hide your feelings. Your body language, your movement and your muscle memory all communicate your true feelings. Your body creates the nervousness you are feeling, which causes stiff arms and makes it virtually impossible to move optimally. So if you're worrying about something in the middle of your swing or stroke or entrance into the water, that movement is likely to be affected. Negatively.

8. Stressing about what other people think of you and your performance.

   "The scouts are in the stands watching me. If I don't play well today the scholarship could be lost."

7. Making unreasonable demands.

   "If I hit another ball into the net, I'm giving my rackets to the first person I see and I'm taking up yoga."

6. Worrying about things you have no control over.

   "If that bird keeps flying around, I just know that my concentration will be ruined and my swing will be horrible."

5. Lack of focus.

   Have you ever been in the middle of an event and realized that you were thinking about the next one. In fact, have you noticed that no matter how important a competition is, you're always thinking about the next one, or even the next day, or what you're going to have for dinner? If you're thinking about what might occur in the future, you're definitely not focusing on the present moment. Your only concern when you are competing should be the present moment.

4. Making a lot of technical errors.

   Hypnosis won't help you if you're not aware of what you're doing. This is why it is important to work with a coach, as your coach is able to see the patterns (good and bad) that you have developed.

   Whether you are using the proper technique or not, the

more you practice, the more patterns you create for your muscles. So if your technique isn't good, when you practice you're creating undesirable patterns in your brain. And the more you've practiced with your bad techniques, the longer and harder it'll be to change them because they've become habits that you are unaware of.

The flipside of all of this, meanwhile, is that if your technique is good and you practice frequently, you have established motor memory (also called muscle memory) that will serve you. Your movements are learned and stored in the brain, which then sends signals to your muscles. The result is that you will not be consciously aware of each movement or feeling, but you'll somehow be doing everything right. You'll be in the zone.

Bad habits are not easy to change without hypnosis. The process of altering them involves being conscious about how you're moving and feeling. It requires concentration on developing new skills to replace the ones you've developed so well that they have become unconscious. And again, it requires the eye of a coach.

If you're trying to develop a new skill, I suggest you practice it for at least 21 days. Anything less will not result in a true learning experience; your desired movement will not become automatic in a couple of days or even weeks.

3. Thinking you're not good enough to be playing at the level you're competing at
   "Maybe I shouldn't be playing in this tournament."

2. Negative self-talk.
   "I'll never hit that ball." And you won't.

1. Allowing past mistakes to consume your thoughts.
   "I always mess up the transition from cycling to running."
   Anxiety prior to performance not only increases negative
   thoughts, but it also negatively affects your coordination.

Here are some exercises and tips that are useful, on the conscious
level, to start reprogramming your mind from expecting more
mistakes to peak performance . . .

- Focus on success. If you have a hard time stopping yourself
  from dwelling in the past, I suggest that you try to focus on
  your past successes rather than mistakes. Visualizing and
  thinking about past successes is an excellent way to build
  confidence and self-esteem. *What you think about is what you
  become.* Therefore, when you concentrate on your successes,
  you help to create future successes.
  When you are completely relaxed and in a highly receptive
  state of mind, repeat the following:

  > *I am grateful for every experience of the past, and for everything
  > connected with those experiences. I find it easy to let go of my
  > fears. I forgive myself for every mistake I have ever made. Life
  > goes on, and so do I: growing rich in experience and in the
  > capacity to achieve. I am stronger than anything life can offer.*

- Mental rehearsal. When you practice your performance in
  your mind, you're doing more than simply visualizing. Use
  all of your senses, be realistic as possible and believe in what
  you see.
- Model excellence. As I've discussed throughout this book,
  modeling is a powerful way to retrain your brain. By

continually imagining the person you want to perform like, and then by putting your face on that person and making them into you in your mind, you have a real, live vision of the performance you desire.

- Embrace change. Resistance to change is a surefire way to exhaust yourself and waste your time. You must love change, desire change, and understand that life *is* change. Change is not positive or negative, it merely *is.* Your reaction to change and your relationship to change are what will determine how easy it is for you to adjust.

- Take time each day to remind yourself of how much you've improved since you first started your sport. Remind your-self of all the positive experiences you have had and all the successes you have achieved. Tell yourself that you are brave, smart, balanced and confident. Tell yourself that you are proud of your achievements and that you believe in your abilities. And, most important of all, remind yourself that each mistake you've made along the way has been a learning experience that has brought you to your current competitive level. When you do something well, tell yourself, out loud, "I did that well." And when you do make a mistake, make sure you look for the things you did well or correctly.

- Be deeply committed to this process. Your Positive Mental Attitude (PMA, a key Napoleon Hill concept) will keep you poised and in a state of equilibrium, and will create an environment where commitment is effortless. When you are constantly seeing and feeling the benefits of commit-ting yourself to attaining the highest level you are capable of, those benefits and that commitment compound. They multiply exponentially (just like negativity and misery compound the more you indulge in them—so beware).

The Importance of Your Mindset

Many athletes develop problems with their mindset because they begin to overindulge in self-criticism and self-judgment. In my experience, athletes are their own worst critics and are very harsh judges.

Early in my career as a hypnotist, I noticed a trend in the athletes that came to me for help with their performance. All of them were extremely talented, and most were already very successful in their sports. They seemed like people who should have been incredibly confident in their abilities. So why were they having trouble with their mindset? I began to see that it had a lot to do with the standards they were setting for themselves.

A poor or weak mindset normally is the result of over-critiquing one's abilities to a fault. It's a result of negative self-judgment. When highly-skilled, successful and otherwise self-confident clients came to see me, I realized that the reason they were having so much trouble with their performance was that they were judging themselves not against other competitors or against their true selves, but against the *unrealistic expectation that they had to perform perfectly each and every time.*

The result of this pressure was counter-productive stress and anxiety that produced negative self-talk and a self-destructive attitude that took away from the quality of their performance.

Gymnasts often believe that it is imperative to do the perfect dismount every time. When they don't perform to their (unreasonable) expectations, they feel frustrated, embarrassed, and humiliated. Their performance can go downhill very fast from there as they start to berate and reject themselves. All of this occurs because they expect perfection.

To overcome the problems that occur because of a poor mindset, I suggest you look at yourself from a brand new perspective. Take a step back and realize that you are in very good company. The best athletes in the world and the most successful players make mistakes all of the time. And they treat them as feedback and they learn from them.

> *"Mistakes are essential to progress. The willingness to learn from them is the backbone of any progress. The object is to succeed, not to count your mistakes."*
> - Tae Yun Kim

Focusing on mistakes creates the fear response I discussed earlier: muscle tension, negative self-talk, inability to concentrate and an accompanying array of other harmful reactions that stand in the way of achieving peak performance.

If you happen to make a mistake, remind yourself that the mistake doesn't reflect on you as a person or an athlete – *it's the way you respond to that mistake that does.* Let me repeat that:

> *Mistakes don't reflect on you as a person or an athlete—the way you respond to them does.*

Joan King, a fellow sports hypnotist and NLP practitioner whose focus is on sports performance, had this to say in one of her seminars several years ago: "Peak performing athletes rarely put themselves down. They talk to themselves positively about what they are attempting to create. They change past negative messages that come up into positive empowering ones. This is a part of their mental training program." She should know.

The bottom line here is that you can be the most important judge of your own performance. The most damaging criticism you can receive is criticism from yourself.

The Importance of Being Confident

The impression we have of who we are and what we might be able to achieve is developed very early in life (many experts say by the age of six). Fortunately, the self-image can be recreated; there are steps you can take to transform your negative self-image into a positive one, and improve your self-confidence:

1. Acknowledge that your self-image is negative and in need of change. Like your realization that your attitude about mistakes needs adjusting, this is the crucial first step in the transformation of your confidence.
2. Make a list of things you like about yourself and your game. Athletic competition can be a powerful tool for improving— or damaging—your self-confidence and self-worth. Notice how rereading the items you like about your game boosts your confidence with each read. Add items each day and reread the entire list each day.
3. Make a list of things you don't like about yourself that cannot be changed. (And then don't spend any more time trying to change them.)
4. Make a list of things you don't like that CAN be changed. (Now here's a great place to focus some energy!).
5. Create a plan for changing the items in #4. (And in Part III: Goal Setting and Achieving, I'll be discussing the process of planning in depth. This is basically my Solutions program, as I noted earlier.) Your confidence will build as you set and achieve your goals and progress on your way to peak performance.

WARNING: There is such a thing as too much confidence. As you know, under-confidence causes negative self-talk and leads to fear of failure, self-doubt and lack of concentration. Naturally, all of this negativity prevents you from enjoying yourself and performing to the best of your ability. But overconfidence is equally dangerous, as it will mislead you into thinking that you and your game can do things that you cannot do. Putting yourself in this impossible situation is not only counterproductive, but it can easily lead to injury, as well.

Designing Peak Performance

Former Brooklyn Dodgers owner Branch Rickey once said, "Luck is the residue of design." In other words, a great way to increase the likelihood of success is to come up with a plan to make it happen. Putting this plan together is a lot simpler than you would imagine, and requires only four steps:

Step 1 is to *know why you are doing what you're doing.* Perhaps you started because your friends do it or you did it in high school. Perhaps you took it up for the mental challenge. Maybe it was the competition that originally attracted you. After spending years practicing and training, however, many people lose sight of their original intent and get caught up in the negative aspects of the competition.

Competing isn't only about winning and losing, it's also about being in touch with yourself and finding your unique talents and abilities. Think of it as a metaphor for empowerment, a metaphor for concentration, a metaphor for the strength we all have but don't think we do.

As soon as you find yourself losing sight of what drew you to your sport in the first place, take a moment and picture how excited you were the first time you had a taste of success.

Remember the sights, sounds, and feelings of that day, and remind yourself how excited and lucky you still are to be involved in such a rewarding sport.

To decide your personal motives for being involved in your sport, ask yourself these questions as often as you can:

- What do I want from it?
- What do I want from myself when I play soccer/run a race/ play golf?
- What do I want *for* myself?

Step 2 is to map out how you plan to get back into the frame of mind you established in Step 1, so that you can enjoy your trip to success. If you've ever used mapquest.com or Yahoo! maps, you know that you can ask the program to create maps or driving directions based on shortest distance in miles, the quickest route, or the most scenic. For your "map," you want to arrive at your destination (success, improvement, winning, having fun) in the easiest and most enjoyable way.

Formulate a plan that you will enjoy executing on a daily and weekly basis. The enjoyment of any kind of sport is in the process of accomplishing, not in the end result itself. I've found throughout my life that the more I enjoy doing something, the more relaxed and confident I am, and the more successful I become at it.

Step 3 is having a way to define and measure your success. How will you know when you've reached your destination? Will it

be when you reach a certain score or win a match or break a
certain time?

Again, think beyond winning and losing. In my CDs I
assume that your goal is to achieve peak performance, and
I show you how to do this through relaxation and mental
imagery exercises that target your subconscious mind. In
many respects, this makes performing at your highest potential as easy and spontaneous as riding a bicycle. Just as the
ability to ride a bike doesn't require conscious thought, once
the keys to relaxed playing are in your subconscious, you
will never again be nervous or question your abilities.

That being said, consider that we've all had days when we've
played extremely well, but for some reason or another didn't
get the result we wanted or thought we deserved. Conversely,
there have been days when our performance fell short of
our own expectations, but we nevertheless did very well. In
which scenario do you experience the most enjoyment?

Keep in mind that the process of becoming a better and
more successful athlete is an ongoing one, and achieving
peak performance simply begins with relaxing and enjoying
yourself while you are performing.

Step 4 is acknowledging your success. If your goal was to win
a particular tournament and you failed, acknowledge the
aspects of your event that were successful. Certainly the
preparation you put into it was a success because you've
matured and developed as a player, trophy or not. There
might be only one winner for each game, race, or match,
but your efforts will lead to another, perhaps bigger win at
another time.

Because of all of the uncontrollable factors in every sport, and because the weather and other variables can vary and many are subjective, you have little control over the results of some of the factors. You do have complete control, however, over the effort you put in, and over what you find enjoyable about your experience.

Let go of negative experiences and bad performances as soon as they occur. The more attention you give them and the more emotion you attach to them, the more prominent a place they will have in your mind and the greater the probability that they will negatively affect your future performance. When a negative thought rises to your conscious awareness, immediately jettison that thought galaxies away, never to return.

Positive experiences and fabulous performances, however, should be remembered in all of their splendor. What do they feel like, sound like, smell like, and look like? Attend to their every detail so you will have a strong mental picture of what you want to replicate in the future.

SELF-HYPNOSIS FOR PEAK PERFORMANCE
INSTANT ALPHA CONDITIONING

Instructions:

1) Use the word you selected to replace the Alpha conditioning technique introduced in *Calm, Cool, & Collected*. Read the following script and let Alpha occur.
2) Then proceed to the script for Peak Performance.

From this moment on, each and every time I desire to attain the deep state of total relaxation, I am instantly and fully relaxed, as I am now drifting into the Alpha state of consciousness. The moment I think my chosen word _____, Alpha occurs. This word has an effect only when I use it and only under the proper circumstances. Each and every time I do use it, I am fully prepared to receive positive, beneficial and constructive suggestions, impressing each one deeper into the storage and memory facility of my brain.

From this moment on, _____ triggers deep relaxation of my mind and body. I feel Alpha occur. I feel wonderful. I feel comfortable. I am totally receptive and responsive to my own creative ideas and suggestions. I am bathed in a glow of quietness, peace and serenity. My chosen word works only when I deliberately use it for deep relaxation to attain Alpha consciousness. Its use in regular conversation has no effect on me whatsoever. From this moment on, each and every time I desire the deep state of total relaxation, I am instantly and fully relaxed upon saying _____. Because my subconscious must follow my command, each and every time I desire total relaxation, I am instantly and fully relaxed when I think my chosen word_____. I feel a deep sense of gratification as this word programming becomes a reality. Feeling wonderful, generous, alive and eager to Achieve Peak Performance.

ACHIEVING PEAK PERFORMANCE

I am talented and skilled at my sport. I am a wonderful person. I take pride in what I do. I am at my very best when I'm engaged in an athletic performance. I am talented and I deserve to be the very best that I can be. I choose to perform at the peak of my abilities. I know that other people appreciate the wonderful skills and abilities that I possess.

I visualize myself performing just like the person I admire most in my sport. When I visualize my role model and admire their natural charisma and natural talent, I know that I can perform with the similar comfort, ease, confidence and skill. I see myself with all of their talent. I believe that I have my role model's skills and strategies. I perform at my peak, just as my role model performs at their peak. I feel my role model's confidence and strength. My athletic performance looks just like my role model's athletic performance.

Every time I compete or practice, I do so with confidence and poise. I perform with the same confidence and the same poise as my role model. I enjoy my sport as much as my role model enjoys it. I am fantastic! I am talented and confident, just like my role model. I know that if they can do it, I can do it! Nothing can stop me from performing at my maximum potential.

I have the motivation and the ability to perform with great confidence and poise. I perform in just the way that I desire. I have the ability to achieve peak performance and therefore I do. I have the confidence and the skills to perform better than I ever have performed before. I become better and better each time I practice or compete.

I completely enjoy what I do. I am a talented and skilled individual. When other people comment on how well I perform to my abilities, I am pleased that they notice my skills. I am most pleased that I have given myself permission to be the best that I can be. I feel fulfilled and accomplished. I feel in control and relaxed. I enjoy myself. I am a gifted athlete. I am better than I ever dreamed possible. Each and every day, with each and every breath that I take, my skills get better and better.

I perform up to my own maximum potential. I listen to my body's common sense limitations and warning signals. With each breath that I take, I feel more confident and better about myself. I am a wonderful person with skills and abilities that I may not even be aware of yet. I am thankful that I discover new and wonderful things about myself each and every day.

I am important to life. I have confidence in my judgment ... I am honest and dependable. My integrity is felt by everyone I meet. I exude radiant vitality and boundless energy. I am courageous and have great faith in myself. I know that I act with complete confidence and poise. I have a wonderful self-image and can do anything I put my mind to.

When I look into a mirror, it is easy for me to say something positive about myself each day. I may focus on my beautiful smile or my glistening eyes. I may acknowledge what a kind person I am. I am thankful that I can say something positive about myself each and every day. As I say positive things about myself, I become more confident.

My mind is a powerful magnet. Whatever I focus on is what I attract into my life. I focus on what I want. I see myself living the life I really want to live. I allow myself to be the best that I can be. I deserve the very best. I allow myself to experience the success that I truly deserve. I take great care of myself. I feel good about myself. I feel relaxed, comfortable, confident and happy. I open my mind to positive thoughts. I believe that I am a winner. I find happiness in life and I enjoy myself. I am a success and I achieve all of my goals. I am always prepared for the next challenge, in sports and in life. I succeed in competition and I deserve to win. My energy is boundless and I feel alive. My confidence radiates to others and my athletic performance is marked by poise and confidence.

This entire suggestion is represented by the letter "M" of my sub-key word "RHYTHM." Anytime I think, say, or see the word "RHYTHM," all suggestions keyed to this word are automatically activated, stimulated and work for my benefit.

You now have the choice to either awaken or to drift off into a normal, natural sleep. If you are going to awaken, say:

Twenty minutes. Wide awake.

If you are going to drift off into a normal, natural sleep, say:

I am now going to drift off into a normal, natural sleep. When I awaken, I will feel fully rested, calm, and at peace with myself, the world and those around me.

Part III

Goal Setting and Achieving

CHAPTER 10

PUTTING IT ALL TOGETHER

Failure to plan is a plan for failure.

GOAL setting and achieving requires dedication, perseverance, and, most important—a plan. In this final chapter, I'll take you through the same step-by-step process I use with my clients to help them achieve peak athletic performance. I'll begin with a question that is deceptively simple to most people: What are outcomes?

Goals Defined

Goals are what you intend to achieve. Sounds simple, right? Well how about this: What's the difference between a goal and a dream? Again, a goal is something you intend to achieve. A dream, on the other hand, is something you'd like to achieve, but for which you don't have a plan. In fact, dreams can be so vaguely worded that they are not easily planned *for.*

Consider Carrie and Matthew:

Carrie: "I want to improve my performance and achieve peak performance."

Matthew: "I will increase my consistency and improve my speed every time I ski moguls within three months."

Who do you think will achieve his or her goal? Clearly, Matthew's goal is more attainable because it is specific and allows for the creation of a timeline, complete with deadlines and action steps. Carrie, on the other hand, words her "goal" so vaguely that it is more like a dream. Wanting something does not imply that you are willing to put in the time and energy necessary to achieve it. Furthermore, Carrie doesn't tell us what constitutes improvement for her or what she would have to do to improve. Everyone wants to achieve peak performance. But people who plan for peak performance will get it, and the people who want it will probably continue to want it for a long time.

Wording Your Goals

Your goals are most useful when they are worded as **outcomes**. There's a lot of confusion around the word "outcome," so if you understand what it is, please bear with me. For the process of achieving peak performance for players, an outcome is a specific, clear statement of what you want to be doing and thinking at the end of a specific timeframe. In other words, "improve my performance" isn't specific enough. What does "improve" look like? Matthew's goal of increasing consistency and speed in three months is a fabulous goal because it is stated as an outcome.

Outcomes must be measurable ("consistency . . . speed . . . in three months") reachable (given Matthew's physical ability, his outcomes are possible), and worded in the positive ("I will . . . "). Remember the discussion of how your brain doesn't know what to do with the word "not," and how it's impossible to not picture, for instance, a purple elephant sitting across from you? Similarly, creating an outcome such as "I will not miss this serve" is a surefire way to miss the serve.

"I am increasing the consistency of my mogul skiing and my speed is improving each time I ski for the next three months." Now that's achievable. That's an outcome!

When creating your own goals, remember . . .

- **The importance of being specific.**
  State your goals as outcomes. Be as specific as possible in describing exactly what it is you will be achieving. Your outcome should be measurable, reachable, and worded in the positive.
- **The importance of a timeframe.**
  Putting a timeframe to your outcomes is what allows you to develop a plan. You might want to travel across the country, but if your timeframe is to do so in one day, that information is going to significantly affect your plan for travel. Goal-setting programs typically categorize your outcomes as short-, mid-, or long-term goals. Short-term is usually one year or less, mid-term is usually 1-5 to ten years, and long-term is anything thereafter. Fortunately you don't have to wait that long to see results with this program.

I use the following timeframes: one month, three months, six months, and one year. So I define short-term goals *as outcomes that will be achieved within one month.* And I use a worksheet that looks something like this:

One Month

  1. Your Physical State

2. Your Inner Monologue
3. Your Focus
4. Your Emotional State
5. Your Mental State
6. Your Expectations

Three Months

1. Your Physical State
2. Your Inner Monologue
3. Your Focus
4. Your Emotional State
5. Your Mental State
6. Your Expectations

Six Months

1. Your Physical State
2. Your Inner Monologue
3. Your Focus
4. Your Emotional State
5. Your Mental State
6. Your Expectations

One Year

1. Your Physical State
2. Your Inner Monologue
3. Your Focus
4. Your Emotional State
5. Your Mental State
6. Your Expectations

- **Your goals will come out of your challenges.**

  Once you have clearly written the challenges you have in each of the six areas I have addressed in the book (i.e., your mental state, your emotional state, your fears, etc.), you will be able to formulate outcomes. The premise here is that of the road map. You must know where your starting point is in order to most effectively reach your destination. Your directions for travel are your plan.

  Based on the above, brief introduction to outcomes, list three outcomes you are going to use this program to achieve. You might revise them later as you gain clarity about the process, so don't be attached to them.

  Outcome #1:_____

  Outcome #2:_____

  Outcome #3:_____

At Summit Performance, I use the ACHIEVE system for outcome creation, planning, and achievement (i.e., what most people refer to as goal setting). It's simple, it's very easy to remember, and you can do it all by yourself in the privacy and comfort of your own home. What clients end up with is a list of Solutions and how to reach them.

The system below takes advantages of hypnosis' ability to turn suggestions into behavior, and NLP's program for manifesting the outcomes you desire. This is where we integrate hypnosis, NLP, and your own unique abilities and wishes, and produce what you have defined for yourself as peak performance.

THE ACHIEVE SYSTEM

A-Action
C- Create
H- Human
I- Identify
E- Energy
V- Value
E- Evaluate

A = ACTION

Before outcomes, before plans, comes something very simple: Deciding that there are things about your performance that you need to change. This is a pivotal moment because that decision is not meaningful until you commit yourself to take **action.**

C = CREATE

To get the outcomes you want, you need to make a plan, right? Well this is where you create your starting point. This is where you define exactly where it is you are right now so that you can develop the most effective, efficient path to where you'd like to go. To create the optimal affirmations and outcomes for yourself, use the following as a guide to creating your starting point. I'll use the example of my client, whom I'll call Debra, to help you understand how this process works.

Why do I need this program?

I'm performing so poorly because I still can't get over that my marriage is failing. I constantly think about it and I'm sure it's partially responsible for how badly I'm doing. And my previous coach and I had a pretty bad falling out and I get so tense whenever she's around that I practically freeze up. I haven't improved at anything and I don't even enjoy playing anymore.

Now you try . . . .

Why do I need this program?

_____

_____

_____

_____

_____

1. Your Physical State

   Debra: Every time I know I'm playing in the presence of my old coach I freeze up. Even worse, all I have to do is *think* about seeing her and I freeze up. She doesn't even have to be there! The anticipation alone is enough to ruin my game. Boy did we end on bad terms, and I have it in my head that she's going to be laughing at me when I play.

   NOW:

   _____

   _____

   _____

   _____

   _____

2. Your Inner Monologue

   Debra: I can't play well enough to play with others. . . . I'll

really screw up when I see my coach. . . . I'm just going to
mess up, I know it. . . . I can't even remember the simplest
things everyone knows how to do sometimes . . . It's so hard
to get even simple things right these days . . . I can't afford
this with everything else going on in my life. . . I can't even
keep my marriage together; I don't know what makes me
think I can compete.

NOW:

_____

_____

_____

_____

_____

3. Your Focus

Debra: My train of thought lately isn't where it's supposed
to be. I try to focus during practice and in competition, but
I think about what else I can do to try to save my marriage.
Then, of course, I'm looking all around for my coach and
imagining what she's thinking about me and how bad I look
these days. I list all of the things I should be doing rather
than trying to compete at my age, too. And the things I need
to do to get my part of the divorce proceedings in order.

NOW:

_____

_____

_____

_____

_____

4. Your Emotional State

Debra: I get so anxious when I have to play. I love playing and I want to play but I get so worried and just can't imagine that I can really do it. . . . I'm so frustrated all the time, and not just with my athletic performance. I'm frustrated about the failure of my marriage, too. It seems that I just can't do anything right. Sometimes it all weighs so heavy on me and it's tough to even get out of bed.

NOW:

_____

_____

_____

_____

_____

5. Your Mental State

Debra: There's so much to think about when you end a 20-year marriage. Sometimes it's overwhelming just listing what I have to do. And I supposedly play sports to relax and have some fun, but it's impossible for me to play well when I am so preoccupied with things other than my game. Then of course there's the dreaded potential encounter with my old coach, which doesn't help my mindset either.

NOW:

_____

_____

_____

---

6. Your Expectations

   Debra: Everyone looks better than I do and is a better player than I am. I've gained weight since my marriage started to fail and that has affected my athletic performance and my attitude, and everything about my playing experience has gone downhill. I'm just not good enough to be doing this anymore.

   NOW:

H = HUMAN

Recognizing your humanity is an integral part of this program. We make mistakes, we have a tendency to be critical and hard on ourselves, we have difficulty forgiving the faults of others as well as ourselves, and have a really hard time releasing bad memories.

Without getting too much into psychoanalysis, much of how we act and react was formulated during childhood. How did your mother or father respond to adversity? Were they competitive? Were they hard on themselves or on you? When did they compete, with whom, and why? How did they respond to others? Were they immediately trusting or not? What did winning mean to them? How did they feel about the person who cut ahead of them in line?

Now how about you? How do you respond to adversity? Are you competitive? Are you hard on your parents or on yourself? With whom do you compete and why? How do you respond to others? Are you immediately trusting or not? What does winning mean to you? How do you feel about the person who cuts ahead of you in line? If your athletic performance is bad, whose fault is it? Yours? Your coach's? The weather? Is there a pattern between your parents and yourself?

If there is, the first part of acknowledging your humanity is to Release and Clear whatever feelings you have about your parents and their influence on who you are today. Let's face it: You can't do anything about the past anyway, so allowing it to adversely affect your thoughts and your performance isn't all that effective as a life strategy.

In addition, reread your responses in the "C=Create" section and note if you are blaming anyone for anything or if you are concentrating on mistakes, bad relationships, or negative feelings from the past. For instance, here was Debra's response:

I need to forgive my soon-to-be ex-husband, my coach, and myself.

What about you?

_____

_____

_____

_____

_____

We all have choices to make every day of our lives. Choosing to be happy and keeping yourself relaxed and calm is one of those decisions. Forgiveness is, too. Let me repeat that: Forgiveness is a conscious decision. Happiness is a conscious decision. Take responsibility for your own state of mind. After all, you're the only one who controls it.

I = IDENTIFY

Now that you've laid the groundwork toward moving past the past, it's time to create the future. It's time to **identify** the affirmations you'll be using throughout whatever time period you choose for your outcomes. Through self-hypnosis, you'll go into Alpha and repeat your affirmations, which compound the effects of your suggestions (i.e., affirmations) so they're even more powerful than when used on the conscious level. You'll find you are able to reach your goals even faster when you combine your effectively written affirmations with the power of autosuggestion.

We'll use Debra's challenges as examples of how you can transform your negative thoughts into a system for changing your behavior and achieving your outcomes.

Your Physical State: From Tense to Relaxed

Debra: Every time I hold the ball (anchor and compounding)
I am calm, I breathe freely and easily and I am completely
relaxed. Each time I see my coach (anchor and
compounding) I feel great about myself. (Remember Natural
Law #1: What you think is what you get.)

Your Inner Monologue: From Negative to Empowering

Debra: Every time I hold my racket (anchor and compounding)
I realize my natural talent and I play tennis well. I easily

recall all of the details from all my practice sessions and my performance is flawless. I visualize myself playing the entire court exactly as it's supposed to be (Theater of the Mind, Natural Law #3: Imagination is more powerful than reality). I enjoy myself and I respond positively to everything I do. (Natural Law #1: What you think is what you get.)

Your Focus: From Scattered to Optimal

Debra: Each time I settle my feet onto the court to prepare to hit the ball, my focus increases (anchor and compounding). I easily stay in the present and all of my concentration is on the task at hand. (Natural Law#1: What you think is what you get.)

(Note: Debra's initial response was to create an affirmation that would help her refrain from thinking about her divorce. Upon attempting to word that affirmation, however, she realized that it was impossible to create one that alluded to NOT thinking about her divorce without actually thinking about her divorce every time. Remember—stick with positive thoughts.)

Your Emotional State: From Apprehensive to Assured

Debra: I am positive and relaxed every time I hold the ball and I easily and quickly reach the zone (anchor and compounding). (Natural Law #2: Every thought causes a physical reaction.) I choose to be happy and look at life in a positive light. (Natural Law 6#: Attitude is a matter of choice.)

Your Mental State: From Terrified to Intrepid

Debra: I am perfectly able to do all of the things I need to do to
prepare for my divorce proceedings. I'll do them in a timely
and orderly fashion, and the proceedings will move ahead
swimmingly because I am so well prepared and so capable
of dealing with everything I must do. (Natural Law #1:
What you think is what you get.) When I see my coach I am
able to play great tennis in a relaxed manner. (Natural Law
#1: What you think is what you get.) I am grateful for the
lessons my coach taught me. (Natural Law #9: Attitude of
gratitude.)

Your Expectations: From Awful to Awesome

Debra: I look fabulous when I play tennis, from my swing, to
my hit, to the way I carry myself as I walk the court. (Natural
Law #1: What you think is what you get; Natural Law #2:
Every thought causes a physical reaction.) Every time I hold
my racket I am confident and self-assured that I can do
anything I put my mind to (anchor and compounding).

E = ENERGY

To cultivate optimal physical abilities you need to have your body
in the best physical condition. This means paying attention to your
energy levels and what affects them.

- Do you get adequate rest?
- Do you eat well?
- Are you getting plenty of exercise?
- Do you avoid negative people?

You need to be aware of how your body responds to your environment and react appropriately to any signals it sends you. When you learn to have complete body-awareness, you are able to perform with more rhythm and fluidity. Remember Natural Law #7: Reactions must be managed. How you react to what is around you affects your health and your performance.

V = VISUALIZE

It's time to make your own home movie out of your outcomes; this is when Theater of the Mind is most helpful. See everything about your outcome, from every angle, including panning around the environment and zooming in on yourself. Zoom in on your match as the spectators are in awe of your performance, and in awe of how calm, cool and collected you are. Feel the excitement of your success.

E = EVALUATE

Evaluation is a critical component to success and should be scheduled into your plan to achieve peak performance. Points of evaluation in your plan allow you to decide if the manner and direction in which you are progressing is acceptable to you. And if it isn't, it gives you the opportunity to regroup and redirect: to chart a different course or use a different strategy and continue in the same direction.

The rationale for building points of evaluation is that those points prevent you from going too far in the wrong direction. If you wait too long to evaluate your plan and your progress, often there is so much wrong with what you are doing that you can't pinpoint the initial place or time when you veered off plan.

This is what I suggest: evaluate your plan and your progress once a week. Decide in advance what progress looks like so you know if you have reached it. It doesn't have to involve anything more sophisticated than a "yes" or a "no."

For example, when Debra was asked to write about one of her goals and how she would evaluate it, she wrote:

In three months my focus and concentration will improve to the point where I am positively affected by the presence of my coach, and I think of my present and future personal life in a positive light. I know that abundance and peak performance are my destiny. I will set the stage for my outcomes by doing Release and Clear everyday, followed by Gaining Concentration, for 21 days. I will practice what my current coach tells me to work on for at least 45 minutes per day, knowing that once I have done what he tells me to do 21 times I will have created a new, more positive habit. When I play competitively in four months, I will enjoy it immensely and I will play better than I ever have.

Debra has created many points for evaluation. Each week, she either did her Release and Clear and Gaining Concentration or she didn't. And she either practiced for 45 minutes or she didn't. These are simple points that demonstrate her commitment to doing the work she needs to do to reach her goals. And if she hasn't done them, she'll know why her goals haven't been reached. As Pat Riley says, "There's no such things as coulda, shoulda, or woulda. If you shoulda and coulda, you woulda done it."

Success is Rarely an Accident

Frank Lloyd Wright once said: "I know the price of success: dedication, hard work and an unremitting devotion to the things you want to see happen." If you have that unrelenting devotion and you are dedicated achieving peak athletic performance, you need to follow the steps of your plan, success will be yours because you believe it already is . . .

A Final Word

ACKNOWLEDGING that you need to change something (or maybe closer to everything!) is the vital first step toward achieving peak athletic performance. And of course, that acknowledgment is the first step, but without follow through results will forever elude you. I think of that trite saying that I used to find very annoying: You get what you pay for. It's true. Your outcome is usually in direct proportion to the amount you were willing to "pay" for it: in energy, in time, in work and in thought.

There is no magic elixir for peak athletic performance. But there is a process that combines the technology of the mind with the teaching of a great coach. As long as the subject (that's you) is willing to do his or her part, the odds of achieving peak performance increase exponentially. Here are my final recommendations:

- Create a journal to not only help you keep track of all of your progress, but to keep track of your thoughts and feelings about taking responsibility for reaching your goals. In addition to monitoring whether you practiced, did your self-hypnosis sessions, and maintained a good attitude, you can respond to the following:

    1) The best part of my practice/game/race/competition today was:

2) My feelings during my lesson or while practicing today were:

3) What I learned about my athletic ability today was:

4) I learned the following about myself today:

5) I learned the following about my coach today:

6) I learned the following about my ability today:

7) I am grateful for these things in my life today:

- Please note that in my experience, the only time optimal results are clearly not forthcoming in this process is when my client doesn't communicate well with his or her coach. Clarify what you are being asked to do—several times if necessary—so you completely understand the whats, whys, and hows of your coach's expectations. If you don't, you'll be sabotaging your own process, and although you'll probably be quick to blame your coach, you will be the one who is ultimately at fault.

- I cannot emphasize enough that you should set standards and goals that are very specific. Those points of progress keep you in check (if you have created them effectively), and you should value your progress so much that you are brimming with pride for your achievements.

The buck stops with you. You owe it to yourself to avail yourself of all of your resources: your coach, your gear and your entire mind and body. I wish you the best and I hope you will give yourself the gift of awesome athletic performance!

Smiling makes you feel good;
it stimulates chemicals in your brain that elevate your mood.
Smile more often!

WORKS CITED

Borysenko, Joan. *Minding the Body, Mending the Mind.* New York: Bantam, 1987.

Carlson, Richard. *You Can Be Happy No Matter What: Five Principles for Keeping Life in Perspective.* Novato: New World, 1997.

Dyer, Wayne W. *The Power of Intention.* Carlsbad: Hay House, 2004.

---. *Manifest Your Destiny: The Nine Spiritual Principles for Getting Everything Want.*

New York: William Morrow, 1998.

Hay, Louise. *You Can Heal Your Life.* Carlsbad: Hay House, 1987.

Hill, Napoleon. *Keys to Success: The 17 Principles of Personal Achievement.* New York: Plume, 1994.

---. *Think and Grow Rich.* New York: Fawcett, 1960.

Kim, Tae Yun. *Seven Steps to Inner Power.* Fremont: Jung SuWon Martial Art Academy, 1991.

Ruiz, Don Miguel. *The Four Agreements Companion Book.* San Rafael: Amber Allen, 2000.

Tolle, Eckhart. *The Power of Now: A Guide to Spiritual Enlightenment.* Novato: New World, 1999.